Charles Dickens

Robert Giddings

GREENWICH EXCHANGE
LONDON

TO THE MEMORY OF GILES GIDDINGS
1964-2002

Greenwich Exchange, London

All rights reserved
Charles Dickens © Robert Giddings 2002

This book is sold subject to the conditions that it shall not, by way of trade or otherwise, be lent, resold, hired out, or otherwise circulated without the publisher's prior consent in any form of binding or cover other than that which it is published and without a similar condition including this condition being imposed on the subsequent publisher.

Printed and bound by Q3 Digital/Litho, Loughborough
Tel: 01509 213456

Typesetting and layout by Albion Associates, London
Tel: 020 8852 4646

Greenwich Exchange Website: www.greenex.co.uk
ISBN 1-871551-26-9

CONTENTS

Chronology

From Boz to Dickens   11

  1 Biographical overview   11
  2 Parental influences   13
  3 Journalism and its influence on Dickens' work   22
  4 Dickens and women   23
  5 Dickens the performer   29

Dickens' Achievement: analysis of the works   33

  1 Early work   34
  2 *Pickwick Papers*   38
  3 *Oliver Twist*   44
  4 *Nicholas Nickleby*   48
  5 *The Old Curiousity Shop*   51
  6 *Barnaby Rudge*   55
  7 *Martin Chuzzlewit*   59
  8 *Dombey and Son*   64
  9 *David Copperfield*   73
 10 *Bleak House*   78
 11 *Hard Times*   84
 12 *Little Dorrit*   86
 13 *Great Expectations*   89
 14 *Our Mutual Friend*   97
 15 Minor works   104

Critical Overview   112

  1 Dickens in modern times   114
  2 Dickens and the dream world   130
  3 Dickens as City correspondent   136
  4 Shades of the prison   148

Selected bibliography and recommended reading   152

For Marie

Acknowledgements

I would like to acknowledge the hours spent talking about Dickens with my friend and colleague, Dr Keith Selby (author of *How to Read a Dickens Novel*) who many a time also helped me sort out my PC.

No book of this kind could ever be written without the London Library.

CHARLES DICKENS 1812 – 1870

Chronology

1812   Charles Dickens born 7 February, Landport, Portsmouth
  – John Dickens moves family to Portsea

1814   John Dickens transferred to London
  – Family moves to Norfolk Street, St Pancras

1815   – Catherine Hogarth (later Dickens' wife) born

1817   Father transferred to Chatham, family moves to Chatham

1821   Goes to William Giles's school, Chatham
  – John Dickens in serious debt, moves family to St Mary's Place, Chatham

1822   John Dickens transferred to London, family moves to Camden Town

1823   Dickens family moves to Gower Street North
  – Mrs Dickens opens school (no pupils)

1824   John Dickens imprisoned for debt (with family in Marshalsea)
  – Dickens works in Warren's Blacking Warehouse, lives at various lodgings
  – Fanny Dickens (his sister) goes to Royal Academy of Music
  – John Dickens released from prison in May
  – Dickens removed from Warren's Blacking, sent to Wellington House Academy

1825   John Dickens retires, moves family to Somers Town, London

1826   John Dickens writing for *The British Press*

1827   John Dickens evicted for non-payment of rates
  – Dickens removed from school, begins work at Ellis and Blackmore, solicitors as clerk
  – Fanny removed from Royal Academy

1828   Works as clerk at Charles Molloy, solicitors
  – John Dickens learns shorthand, works for *Morning Herald*

1829   John Dickens moves family to Norfolk Street, Fitzroy Square
  – Dickens learns shorthand, works as reporter at Doctors' Commons

1830   Dickens meets Maria Beadnell
  – Becomes reader at British Museum

1831   Meets John Forster
  – Reporting for *Mirror of Parliament*

1832   Dickens courting Maria Beadnell
  – Reporting for *True Sun*

1833   Dickens' first story published ('A Dinner at Poplar Walk' in *Monthly Magazine*)
  – Romance with Maria Beadnell terminated
  – John Dickens moves family to Bentinck Street

1834 Dickens has eight more stories published in *Monthly Magazine*
- Meets Catherine Hogarth
- John Dickens arrested for debt
- Dickens reporter for *Morning Chronicle*
- Five Sketches published in *Morning Chronicle*
- Stories commissioned for *Evening Chronicle*
1835 Twenty Sketches published in *Evening Chronicle*
- Engaged to Catherine Hogarth
1836 First Series of *Sketches by Boz* published
- Begins *Pickwick Papers* (serialised March 1836 to October 1837)
- Marries Catherine Hogarth, at St Luke's, Chelsea
- Couple live at Furnival's Inn, with Fred Dickens and Mary Scott Hogarth
- Hablot Browne ('Phiz') becomes his illustrator
- *Strange Gentleman* and *Village Coquettes* produced at St James's Theatre
- *Sketches by Boz*, Second Series published
1837 Charles Culliford Boz Dickens born
- Begins writing *Oliver Twist* (serialised February 1837 to March 1839)
- Mary Hogarth dies suddenly
- Writing *Pickwick* and *Oliver Twist* suspended for a month
- Dickens introduced to William Charles Macready by Forster
- Holidays in Belgium with Hablot Browne
1838 Goes to Yorkshire to investigate Yorkshire schools
- Mary ('Mamie') Dickens born
- Begins *Nicholas Nickleby* (serialised April 1838 to October 1839)
- Visits Midlands, North and Wales
1839 Visits Manchester with Forster and Harrison Ainsworth
- Begins *Barnaby Rudge*
1840 Visits Walter Savage Landor with Forster at Bath
- Visits Birmingham, Stratford-on-Avon and Lichfield with Catherine and Forster
- Begins *The Old Curiosity Shop* (serialised April 1840 to February 1841)
- *Master Humphrey's Clock* appears (to December 1841)
1841 Walter Landor Dickens born
- Dickens finishes *The Old Curiosity Shop*
- Serialisation of *Barnaby Rudge* begins (February 1841 to November 1841)
- Dickens and Catherine visit Scotland
- Writing *Master Humphrey's Clock*

1842 Dickens and Catherine visit USA
  – Campaigns for international copyright
  – Writing *American Notes* (published October)
  – Begins writing *Martin Chuzzlewit*
1843 Rents farm in Finchley to concentrate on writing *Chuzzlewit* (serialised January 1843 to July 1844)
  – Family holiday at Broadstairs
  – Writing *A Christmas Carol* (published, December 1843)
1844 Francis Jeffrey Dickens born
  – Writing *The Chimes* (published December)
  – Reads *The Chimes* to friends in London
1845 Dickens family in Genoa (until June)
  – Writes *The Cricket on the Hearth* (published December)
  – Alfred D'Orsay Dickens born
  – Appears in Beaumont and Fletcher's *The Elder Brother* at Fanny Kelly's Theatre
  – Family return from Italy
1846 Edits *Daily News* (January)
  – *Pictures From Italy* serialised in *Daily News*
  – Resigns editorship of *Daily News* 9 February
  – Begins writing *Dombey and Son* (June)
  – *Battle of Life* published (December)
  – *Dombey and Son* begins serialisation (October 1846 until April 1848)
1847 Sydney Smith Haldimand Dickens born
  – Dickens in performances of *Every Man in his Humour* (and other plays) at Manchester and Liverpool
1849 Dickens family stay in Brighton (serialisation of *David Copperfield*, May 1849 to October 1850)
  – Henry Fielding Dickens born
1850 Begins *Household Words*
  – *Copperfield* Dinner at Richmond
  – Visits France with Maclise
  – Dora Annie Dickens born (dies in infancy)
  – Performs in *Every Man in His Humour* at Knebworth
1851 Performs in plays at Rockingham Castle
  – Catherine suffers nervous collapse
  – John Dickens (father) dies
1852 Edward Bulwer Lytton Dickens born
  – Tours with *Not So Bad As We Seem* (with Catherine)
  – Serialisation of *Bleak House* (March 1852 to September 1853)

1854   Travels to Preston
        – Views strike at Boulogne
        – Begins *Hard Times* (serialised April to August 1854)
1855   In Paris with Wilkie Collins
        – Meets (Mrs Winter) Maria Beadnell again
        – Begins *Little Dorrit* (serialised December 1855 to June 1857)
1856   Buys Gad's Hill Place
1857   Acts in the *Frozen Deep* at Tavistock House, and at Gallery of
        Illustration
        – Meets and falls in love with Ellen Ternan
        – Walter Dickens leaves for India
        – Serious discord with Catherine Dickens begins
        – Tours in *The Frozen Deep* (with Ellen Ternan)
1858   Begins public readings
        – Separates from Catherine
1859   *All the Year Round* begins publication
        – Begins *A Tale of Two Cities* (published April to November 1859)
1860   Begins articles, *The Uncommercial Traveller* in *All The Year Round*
        – Begins writing *Great Expectations* (serialised December 1860 to
        August 1861)
        – Gives up Tavistock House, now settled at Gad's Hill
1861   Establishes pied-à-terre at Hanover Terrace, Regent's Park
        – Sydney Dickens appointed to *HMS Orlando*
        – Begins second series of readings
1862   Current reading tour ends at Chester
        – Georgina Hogarth ill. Takes her and Mamie Dickens to Paris
1863   Returns to Paris with Georgina and Mamie
        – Gives readings in Paris and London
        – Begins writing *Our Mutual Friend*
        – Death of his mother
        – Death of Walter Dickens in India
1864   Frank Dickens leaves for India
        – Serialisation of *Our Mutual Friend* (May 1864 to November 1865)
        – At Gad's Hill from June
1865   Suffers lameness, early symptoms of thrombosis
        – Holidays in Paris, with Ellen Ternan
        – 9 June in serious railway accident, Staplehurst, Kent. He is uninjured
        but very shaken
1866   – Suffers from heart trouble and other forms of ill health
        – Undertakes further 30 readings, April to June, beginning at Liverpool

1867 Symptoms of exhaustion, faintness, fear of rail travel
   – Begins new series of 50 readings January to May, beginning at Liverpool
   – Plans American tour, despite swollen foot and other ailments
   – 9 November, sails for America. First reading in Boston
1868 Continues American tour, despite failing health
   – April, Farewell Readings at Boston and New York. Sails for England
   – Health improved, entertains friends at Gad's Hill
   – Edward Bulwer Dickens (youngest son) sails for Australia
   – Farewell reading tour planned
   – Writes and works up *Sikes and Nancy Murder*
1869 Readings resume. *Sikes and Nancy Murder* read in public
   – On medical advice he abandons readings
1870 Lives at Hyde Park place, regularly visits Ellen Ternan at Windsor Lodge, Peckham
   – Suffers pain in left hand and failure in left eye
   – Begins *The Mystery of Edwin Drood*
   – Begins Farewell Readings at St James's Hall
   – Serialisation of *Edwin Drood* (begins April, ends at his death in June)
   – Last farewell reading in London in March
   – Dies 9 June
   – Buried at Poets' Corner, Westminster Abbey on 14 June

FROM BOZ TO DICKENS

1 Biographical overview

> No one thinks first of Mr Dickens as a writer. He is at once, through his books, a friend. He belongs among the intimates of every pleasant-tempered and large-hearted person. He is not so much the guest as the intimate of our homes. He keeps holidays with us, he helps us to celebrate Christmas with heartier cheer, he shares at every New Year in our good wishes: for, indeed, it is not in his purely literary character that he has done most for us, it is as a man of the largest humanity, who has simply used literature as the means by which to bring himself into relations with his fellow-men.
>
> Charles Eliot Norton, in *North American Review*, April 1868

Charles Dickens is an exception to the general rule that an author's life is not as interesting as their work. Details of Dickens' life continue to be discovered, the publication of his complete letters has aroused great interest in recent years and there have been several well documented modern biographies.

I shall explore those areas of his life that I believe had the greatest influence on his professional authorship – his childhood experiences, journalism, his erotically troubled life. I shall also explore, briefly, Dickens as a performer of his own work.

Charles Dickens was born on 7 February 1812 at Landport, Portsmouth, where his father, John Dickens, was a clerk in the Navy Pay Office. Charles was a sensitive boy and his haphazard schooling and harrowing spell in Warren's Blacking Warehouse are movingly recycled in the opening chapters of *David Copperfield*. Dickens based Wilkins Micawber closely on John Dickens. The novelist idealised childhood in his fiction: some find his suffering children insufferable. Nevertheless, the young Dickens had the chance to read the major classics of the 18th century in his father's collection of Fielding, Defoe, Smollett, Goldsmith – literary experiences which marked the novelist for life. He was also taken frequently to the theatre, which intoxicated him. Towards the end of his professional life he became a public performer of his own works.

Soon after the family moved to London John Dickens was imprisoned for debt (and his family with him). These experiences resurface in *Little Dorrit*.

When he left school he began work as a solicitor's clerk. He read voraciously and learned shorthand. He then became a parliamentary reporter and worked for several newspapers, travelling over the country covering elections, experiences of much value to him in *Pickwick Papers*. He began to contribute short stories to periodicals – collected as *Sketches by Boz*.

At this time he met and fell head over heels in love with Maria Beadnell, the pretty and capricious daughter of a banker. She passed him over, but was the prototype for several flirtatious characters, notably Dolly Varden in *Barnaby Rudge*. He met and married Catherine, daughter of George Hogarth, a fellow journalist.

Serial publication, an inexpensive method of marketing lengthy fiction, was fast becoming the accepted means of literary production. Publishers were looking for writers such as Dickens who could write satisfactory fiction, apparently to order, in serial form. His reputation as a skilful writer was burgeoning and he was asked to write the copy to accompany pictures illustrating the adventures of a group of Cockney sportsmen. The result was the sensationally successful *Pickwick Papers*. Suddenly he was famous and rapidly commissioned to write *Oliver Twist, Nicholas Nickleby, Barnaby Rudge*. He planned *Master Humphrey's Clock*, as a series of miscellaneous stories, but the popularity of the story of Nell and her grandfather overtook the project and took readers by storm as *The Old Curiosity Shop*.

He visited USA in 1841 and published *American Notes* on his travels, also using American episodes to increase the flagging sales of *Martin Chuzzlewit* in 1843-4. The *Christmas Books*, including the story of Scrooge in the immortal *A Christmas Carol*, appeared in the mid 1840s. He was briefly editor of the *Daily News* and then began *Dombey and Son* 1846-8. *David Copperfield*, a deeply autobiographical novel, followed soon after. He was extremely busy, in amateur theatricals, writing and running the journal *Household Words*. *Bleak House, Hard Times, Little Dorrit* and *A Tale of Two Cities* appeared during the 1850s. At the same time he began public readings of his own works. He began another periodical, *All the Year Round*, in 1859.

While putting Wilkie Collins's melodrama, *The Frozen Deep*, into production Dickens met the young actress Ellen Ternan. By this time his relationship with Catherine Dickens was considerably strained.

Some idea of his state of mind can be gauged from this letter:

> I believe that no two people were ever created, with such an impossibility of interest, sympathy, confidence, sentiment, tender union of any kind between them, as there is between my wife and me. It is an immense misfortune to her – it is an immense misfortune to me – but Nature has put an insurmountable barrier between us, which never in this world can be thrown down. …she is the only person whom I have ever known with whom I could not get on somehow or other, and in communicating with whom I could find some way to come to some kind of interest. You know that I have many compulsive faults which often belong to my impulsive way of life and exercise of fancy; but I am very patient and considerate at heart, and would have beaten out a better journey's end than we have come to, if I could…

Ellen Ternan was a very pretty girl, with fair hair, blue eyes and a lively personality, who looked younger than her eighteen years. She had large blue eyes and golden curly hair which hung in ringlets. Dickens fell madly, intoxicatingly and indulgently in love with her.

Great Expectations and *Our Mutual Friend* were published in the early 1860s while his public readings were in full swing, including a tour of the USA, which netted him a fortune. He was suffering from severe strain and on medical advice he attempted to slacken his pace. In 1869 he began work on *The Mystery of Edwin Drood*, but died in June 1870 with only a few chapters written.

2   Parental influences

Charles Dickens' father was an irresponsible, loquacious and unambitious man of considerable charm. Charles always held him in great affection. John Dickens was an insecure member of the lower non-professional middle-class, with genteel but unrealisable aspirations. Consequently the family was always in debt. Frequent removals to escape rent arrears and other debts were a feature of the Dickens' family life. Robert Langton, who knew John Dickens in his later years, described him as a talkative, pleasant companion:

...possessing a varied fund of anecdotes and a genuine vein of humour. He was a well-built man, rather stout, of very active habits, a little pompous... He dressed well, and wore a goodly bunch of seals suspended across his waistcoat from his watch and chain.

The Childhood and Youth of Charles Dickens, 1891

He was very long-winded. Langton records that he would say such things as: "I must express my tendency to believe that his longevity is (to say the least of it) extremely problematical" rather than "I do not think he will live long." Charles used aspects of his father for Wilkins Micawber in *David Copperfield*:

> ...I am at present, my dear Copperfield, engaged in the sale of corn upon commission. It is not an avocation of a remunerative description – in other words, it does not pay – and some temporary embarrassments of a pecuniary nature have been the consequence. I am, however, delighted to add that I have now an immediate prospect of something turning up (I am not at liberty to say in what direction), which I trust will enable me to provide, permanently, both for myself and for your friend Traddles, in whom I have an unaffected interest...

A sinister version of these characteristics is discernible in William Dorrit, the Father of the Marshalsea in *Little Dorrit*.

Although by some accounts, a loving and affectionate parent, the novelist came to despise his mother as a silly, affected, vain, scatterbrained person, and cruelly guyed her in the person of Mrs Nickleby:

> I had a cold once... I think it was in the year eighteen hundred and seventeen; let me see, four and five are nine, and – yes, eighteen hundred and seventeen, that I thought I never should get rid of... I was only cured at last by a remedy that I don't know whether you ever happened to hear of... You have a gallon of water as hot as you can possibly bear it, with a pound of salt and sixpenn'orth of the finest bran, and sit with your head in it for twenty minutes every night just before going to bed; at least, I don't mean your head – your feet. It's a most extraordinary cure. I used it for the first time, I recollect, the day after Christmas Day, and by the middle of April following the cold was gone. It

seems quite a miracle when you come to think of it, for I had it ever since the beginning of September...

Later, when she read *Nicholas Nickleby*, Dickens' mother asked him if such a person really could have existed. He did not tell her. Nevertheless it was his mother who actually taught him to read, planting the first seeds of what was to be a vast harvest.

Kent: haven of the imagination

The young Dickens was absorbing visual impressions of his environment. His father took him for walks around the Kent landscape – Frindlesbury, Chequers Street, Chalk, Cobham, the Canterbury-Dover road, Snorridge Bottom, Rochester and Gad's Hill, where there was an in impressive bay-windowed red brick house, with a portico, mansard roof and bell tower. This was Gad's Hill Place, and Dickens loved it and eventually came to own it. His father said to him: "If you were to be very persevering, Charles, and were to work hard, you might some day come to live in it." The Pickwickians' early travels and adventures occur in Kent. Samuel Pickwick notes of Strood, Rochester, Chatham and Brompton:

> The principal production of these towns... appear to be soldiers, sailors, Jews, chalk, shrimps, officers, and dockyard men. The commodities chiefly exposed for sale in the public streets are marine stores, hard-bake, apples, flat fish, and oysters. The streets present a lively and animated appearance, occasioned chiefly by the conviviality of the military. It is truly delightful to a philanthropic mind to see these gallant men staggering along under the influence of an overflow, both of animal and ardent spirits...
>
> *Pickwick Papers*, Chapter 2

A comic antiquarianism of the Rochester locality is provided in deft brush strokes in the pointillistic verbal telegraph English of Mr Jingle:

> Ah! Fine place... glorious pile – frowning walls – tottering arches – dark nooks – crumbling staircases – old cathedral too...
>
> ibid

Mr Jingle also provides the famous tag line of Kent as the English paradise: "Everybody knows Kent – apples, cherries, hops, and women."

(ibid Chapter 2.) When the brutalised young David Copperfield is finally driven to run away, all his hopes of salvation are located in Kent. On his six day flight to his Aunt Betsy Trotwood's house on the Downs outside Dover he is sustained by hope: Kent and its associations bear him up, his constant thoughts are of the hops, the sunny streets of Canterbury, the sight of its old houses and gateways "and the stately, grey Cathedral, with the rooks sailing round the towers" (*David Copperfield* Chapter 13). Throughout his life, these childhood impressions of Kent were the haven of Dickens' imagination.

Wandering the streets
When the family moved to London, Dickens took to wandering about the streets of Camden and Kentish Town. He even got as far as Holborn and the City. He gained satisfaction simply from wandering and observing the multiplicity of activities – people, shops, businesses, traffic, warehouses, counting-houses, dock-buildings, shipyards, taverns, theatres, archways, sailors' homes, ship-breakers' yards, second-hand clothes dealers', cook-shops, doss-houses, courts, alleys, little squares, timber-sheds, chandlers – which made up life in the metropolis. This was a habit which remained with him for the rest of his life.

He thus gained that extraordinarily rich, intimate knowledge of London which powerfully informs and enlivens so much of his fiction. He was clearly fascinated by the contrasts of busy metropolitan life, where the riches of the world were displayed amid the grimmest poverty:

> ...Emporiums of splendid dresses, the materials brought from every quarter of the world; tempting stores of everything to stimulate and pamper the sated appetite and give new relish to the oft-repeated feast; vessels of burnished gold and silver, wrought into every exquisite form of vase and dish, and goblet; guns, swords, pistols, and patent engines of destruction; screws and irons for the crooked, clothes for the newly-born, drugs for the sick, coffins for the dead, churchyards for the buried – all these each jumbled with the other and flocking side by side... The rags of the squalid ballad-singer fluttered in the rich light that showed the goldsmith's treasures; pale and pinched-faces hovered about the windows where was tempting food; hungry eyes wandered over the profusion guarded by one thin sheet of brittle glass – an iron wall to them; half-naked shivering figures stopped to gaze at Chinese shawls and golden stuffs of India.

There was a christening party at the largest coffin-maker's, and a funeral hatchment had stopped some great improvements in the bravest mansion. Life and death went hand in hand; wealth and poverty stood side by side; repletion and starvation laid them down together. But it was London...

Nicholas Nickleby, Chapter 32

Warren's Blacking

By 1823 John Dickens' fecklessness began to catch up with him. Creditors began seriously to press for their money. Charles' mother resolved to come to the family's assistance and so she opened a school. Despite an imposing brass doorplate and efficient local pamphletting, no pupils enrolled. (The experience is revisited as Mrs Micawber's Boarding Establishment for Young Ladies in *David Copperfield*). Items of furniture were sold. Visits were made to pawnbrokers. Charles now lost the precious collection of books he had found so consoling. His education was neglected. But things were to get even worse.

Every financial assistance was needed for the family. Charles was sent to work. Through a distant relative employment was found for the 12 year old boy at Warren's Blacking Warehouse, Hungerford Stairs (now beneath Charing Cross Station). For six shillings a week he pasted labels on the bottles of grate blacking. He had scarcely been at this employment two weeks when his father was arrested for debt.

Even before his father had been arrested, Charles had felt utterly neglected and treated like a drudge at home. His parents seemed to take no interest in him nor consider what might be done to secure his future. There had been no second thoughts about sending him out to earn a few shillings. And now here he was, cast out into the world, living his working life like a premature adult. The contrast lay between his expectations and the reality of life – child labour was a commonplace of British 19th century working life, but not to one of the class to which he thought he belonged.

These episodes constitute recurring configurations of experience in his fiction – in the Micawbers, in Trent's neglect of Little Nell, in the death of Smike, in Dombey's neglect of his daughter Florence, and the terrible story of the Dorrit family. His fiction is full of the echoes of the blacking factory – Tony Weller in *Pickwick* mocks the kind of verses used to advertise Warren's Blacking. Mr Slum, the commercial muse employed by Mrs Jarley's Waxworks in *The Old Curiosity Shop* is a further satiric attack on the exploitation of verse for advertising purposes. In

17

Great Expectations Joe Gargery makes a point of going to see Warren's Blacking Warehouse when he visits London. Towards the end of his life, playing a memory game with his children, Dickens mysteriously incorporated 'Warren's Blacking' into a string of nonsense to be committed to memory and passed on to the next player.

Whatever his mother and father thought about these terrible days, and the part they played in them, they did not ever mention it again. In the account he gave to his close friend John Forster (who was his first biographer) he wrote:

> I have no idea how long it lasted; whether for a year, or much more, or less. From that hour, until this, my father and my mother have been stricken dumb upon it. I have never heard the least allusion to it... from either of them...
>
> John Forster: *The Life of Charles Dickens*, 1872

The account is an extraordinary personal document, very revealing of Dickens' deep anguish at the memory of those terrible days:

> I (small Cain that I was, except that I had never done harm to anyone) was handed over as a lodger to a reduced old lady... in Little College Street, Camden Town, who took children in to board... She had a little brother and sister under her care then; somebody's natural children... and a widow's little son. The two boys and I slept in the same room. My own exclusive breakfast, of a penny cottage loaf, and a pennyworth of milk, I provided for myself. I kept another small loaf, and a quarter pound of cheese, on a particular shelf... to make my supper when I came back at night. They made a hole in the six shillings I know well; and I was out at the blacking factory all day, and had to support myself upon that money all the week... No advice, no counsel, no encouragement, no consolation, no support, from anyone that I can call to mind, so help me God... Sundays, Fanny and I passed in the prison... I was so young and childish, and so little qualified... to undertake the whole charge of my own existence, that... I could not resist the stale pastry put out at half-price on trays at the confectioners' doors in Tottenham Court Road; and I often spent the money I should have kept for dinner... When I had no money, I took a turn in Covent Garden market, and stared at the pine-apples... I know I do not exaggerate... the scantiness of my resources and the difficulties of my life... I know that I

worked, from morning to night, with common men and boys, a shabby child. I know that I tried... not to anticipate my money, and to make it last the week through; by putting it away in a drawer...wrapped into little parcels, each parcel containing the same amount, and labelled with a different day...

A closed book

On 2 March 1824, Dickens' father applied for retirement from the Admiralty Pay Office on grounds of ill health. Then, in April, John Dickens' mother died and he inherited £450. The novelist's father handed this sum over to his creditors. On 28 May, after coming to an arrangement with his creditors, John Dickens was allowed to leave prison under the Insolvent Debtors Act. He retired in March the following year on the grounds of ill health – he suffered chronic infection of the urinary organs. He was granted a pension of £146 a year. John Dickens then began a new career – in journalism. By November 1826 he finally cleared his debts. This was a propitious period in the future development of Charles Dickens. His father had already shown enterprise and by having a report of the Chatham fire of 1820 published in *The Times* and he was now a correspondent of the *British Press*.

Charles probably now hoped that he would taken away from the blacking factory and sent back to school. However, he was not immediately to be released from his servitude at Warren's Blacking. The firm was doing well and had moved its premises to the corner of Chandos Street and Bedford Street, and Charles and a companion worked in the window overlooking Bedford Street where they were often stared at by passers-by. This may have led to words between the boy's father and his employer. John Dickens might not altogether have approved of his son's making such an exhibition of himself. Charles was suddenly compelled to leave this employment.

His servitude was at an end but his mother was not at all pleased. Aware how short they would be with Charles' wages gone, she was anxious things should be patched up and that Charles go back to Warren's shop. John Dickens wouldn't hear of it. In June 1824 Charles was sent to school at Wellington House Academy, and wept with gratitude. These were early days in press reporting and his father urged him to bring him possible news stories of such likely subjects as fires, accidents, law reports. Payment was a penny a line. Eventually Charles himself was to become a journalist.

The blacking factory episode was closed. The entire matter remained a secret, deeply locked inside Charles Dickens. He kept the memory of these events to himself: he did not tell his wife, Catherine, nor family, nor friends – however close – until the secret was accidentally disclosed and he told John Forster in 1847.

His fiction is full of people with secrets. Mr Bounderby is destroyed when the secrets of his past life are exposed. As Pip in *Great Expectations* says; "...the secret was such an old one now, had grown into me and become part of myself, that I could not tear it away..." Mrs Clennam in *Little Dorrit* is tortured by her secret past. The Father of the Marshalsea Prison has a mental relapse and reveals the appalling secrets of his past at a social dinner. Lady Dedlock carries a dreadful secret in her heart in *Bleak House*. Dr Mannette in *A Tale of Two Cities* has a whole past life locked in his memory. Mr Nadget in *Martin Chuzzlewit* is such a secret person he writes mysteriously to himself. The memories of the blacking factory went everywhere with Dickens. Prisons, prisoners, guilt-racked figures, blacking bottles, blacking brushes, boot blacking advertisements, blacking warehouses recur throughout the fiction as a personally coded discourse. The now famous autobiographical fragment he gave to John Forster is among the most remarkable passages he ever wrote. It is only by understanding what this experience meant to him that we can ever hope to understand the neverending search for love which dominated him. He was forced to work before his time and compelled to work in degrading conditions in company he found uncongenial. As far as he could see, his parents expressed no regret nor raised protest about these reduced circumstances. His mother, it seemed to him, was all for his being sent to work. All that he thought comforting and consoling in life was suddenly torn from him and he was mercilessly exposed to the harshest humiliations life could offer. Family, friends, home-life, school-companions, innocence, fun – all evaporated like an insubstantial dream. His only value to anyone resided in the money he could be made to earn. To see this as he must have seen it is to understand his almost unsatiable need for demonstrative, unconditional love.

This sense of anguish haunted his adult life. He felt his marriage empty and sought sexual love elsewhere. He demanded (and maintained) the loyalty of readers. He strove to earn the apparent rewards of plentiful money, and when he acted in plays he responded almost physically to the applause of the audience – "There's nothing in the world equal to seeing the house rise at you, one sea of delighted faces, one hurrah of applause" he told Mary Cowden Clarke (*Recollections of Writers*, 1878 p324). He sought to earn the adoration of the public at his readings, to the extent that it nigh on killed him. As Charles Dolby, his manager said: "setting aside his pecuniary profits, the pleasure he derived from this (the reading tours) is not to be told in words" (Charles Dolby: *Charles Dickens as I Knew Him: The Story of the Reading Tours 1866-1870*, 1885, p451).

His fiction is full of isolated, deprived or neglected children – Oliver Twist, Smike, Nell, Paul and Florence Dombey, David Copperfield, Pip, Amy Dorrit. And so much of his fiction is a search for perfect love and ideal companionship. Children are his saints. Adults who represent work, money and figures – the fundamentals of economic life – are the villains of the Dickens world. There are saintly adults, but they are such as the world itself would consider unreasonable, (often illiterate), illogical people – semi-idiots – such as Newman Noggs, Tom Pinch, Bob Cratchit, Captain Cuttle, Mister Dick, Joe Gargery. But these children in adult shape are the ones who show love and offer help. The sensible, worldly people, such as society would admire and consider successful, these numerate and orthodox people seem to Dickens symbolic of the evil materialism of the world; Mr Dombey is associated with his ticking watch but Cuttle's watch won't even tell the correct time. Joe can't read, but Pumplechook sets Pip an endless series of oral practical arithmetic problems all the way to Satis House. The folly of the world, and the wisdom of childhood are the basic lessons Scrooge has to learn.

These pre-adolescent experiences constantly resurface in his work. When he writes about the inhumanity of modern society, he is also writing about himself.

3   Journalism and its influence on Dickens' work

In his own words:

> I went into the gallery of the House of Commons as a Parliamentary reporter when I was a boy of not eighteen, and left it – I can hardly believe the inexorable truth – nigh thirty years ago. I have pursued the calling of a reporter under circumstances of which many of my brethren at home in England here, many of my modern successors, can form no adequate conception. I have often transcribed for the printer from my shorthand notes, important public speeches in which the strictest accuracy was required, and a mistake in which would have been to a young man severely compromising, writing on the palm of my hand, by

the light of a dark lantern, in a post chaise and four, galloping through a wild country, all through the dead of night, at the then surprising rate of fifteen miles an hour. The very last time I was at Exeter, I strolled into the Castle Yard there to identify... the spot on which I once 'took', as we used to call it, an election speech of my noble friend Lord Russell (speech by Russell on 1 May 1835) in the midst of a lively fight maintained by all the vagabonds in that division of the county, and under such a pelting rain, that I remembered two good-natured colleagues, who chanced to be at leisure, held a pocket handkerchief over my notebook after the manner of a state canopy in an ecclesiastical procession. I have worn my knees by writing on them on the old back row of the old gallery of the old House of Commons; and I have worn my feet where we used to be huddled together like so many sheep kept in waiting, say, until the woolsack might want re-stuffing. I have been, in my time, belated on miry roads, towards the small hours, in a wheelless carriage, with exhausted horses and drunken postboys, and have got back in time for publication, to be received with never-forgotten compliments by the late Mr Black (John Black, editor of *The Morning Chronicle*) coming in the broadest of Scotch from the broadest of hearts I ever knew...

After the publication of *Sketches by Boz* he was able to move from being a successful and productive hack, into successful authorship. His father in law, George Hogarth, introduced him to Richard Bentley, a successful publisher, and in the summer of 1836 Bentley offered to him £400 each for two novels. With the success of *Pickwick Papers* an undoubted fact, he wrote to Bentley:

I have spoken to some confidential friends... They concur in thinking, and strongly advise me, that for the copyright of a Novel in Three Volumes, I should have Five Hundred Pounds... considering the time, the labour, the casting about, in every direction, for materials: the anxiety I should feel to make it a work on which I might build my fame and the great probability of its having a very large sale (we are justified in forming our judgement upon the rapid sale of everything I have yet touched) I think you will not object to raising your terms thus far... Recollect that you are dealing with an Author not quite unknown, but who, so far as he has gone, has been most successful...

Letter dated 17 August 1836

We can see immediately that the attributes of journalism – keen observation, fast writing under constrained circumstances, knowing what the public wants to hear and a keen eye on commercial value – are already in place. Remarkably, at the same time he is able to use this treacherous form of writing – he could easily be led into writing trash to please the public – to write what he passionately felt to be true. In no other writer do we find the journalistic use of feedback from public reaction to literary form to be so explicit. This was both the achievement and limitation of his work. After some negotiations he was able to leave the *Morning Chronicle* to devote himself to full time authorship. He was no longer a hack. He was writing novels and was to edit his own periodicals.

4   Dickens and women

If we are seeking to explain the bewildering stereotyping of women in his fiction, we can at least shed some light on this by exploring what we know of his own relationships with women.

He loved his mother, but her actions towards him which we have already explored caused him to be fiercely critical of her and unforgiving. He is like a disappointed 'lover' who has been rejected. And he exacts his vengeance by showing the world what his mother was like, and for Dickens this means caricature and ridicule. The pattern is repeated in the case of Maria Beadnell. Again he is smitten only to be rejected. She too gets the treatment as the immortal Dolly Varden in *Barnaby Rudge*: "a roguish face… a face lighted up by the loveliest pair of sparkling eyes… the face of a pretty, laughing girl; dimpled and fresh, and healthful – the very impersonation of good-humour and blooming beauty" and Dora "…She had the most delightful little voice, the gayest little laugh, the pleasantest and most fascinating little ways, that ever led a lost youth into hopeless slavery…" in *David Copperfield*.

He was to meet Maria again in 1854 – she was now the fat and empty-headed Mrs Winter – and she is cruelly portrayed as Flora Finching:

> Flora, always tall, had grown to be very broad too, and short of breath; but that was not much. Flora, whom he had left a lily, had become a peony; but that was not much. Flora, who had seemed enchanting in all she said and thought, was diffuse and silly. That

was much. Flora, who had been spoiled and artless long ago, was determined to be spoiled and artless now. That was a fatal blow.

Little Dorrit

In 1834 Dickens became acquainted with George Hogarth, a fellow journalist with the *Morning Chronicle*. Dickens got to know the Hogarth family who loved him as he was so full of fun and willing to join in whatever was going on. He was soon captivated by Kate, a buxom lass with glossy dark hair, blue eyes, full lips, a slightly retroussé nose and ready humour. She enjoyed Dickens' company enormously. Her younger sister, Mary Scott Hogarth, who was fifteen, looked up to him. In the spring of 1835 Catherine and Charles were engaged. The family was delighted.

Charles Dickens and Catherine Hogarth were married at St Luke's, Chelsea, on 2 April 1836 and spent their honeymoon at Chalk, near Gravesend. They returned to set up home at Furnival's Inn, with Dickens' brother, Fred. Significantly, Mary Hogarth was such a constant visitor that she was almost part of the household. Dickens was busy writing *Pickwick* while still doing parliamentary reporting.

God seemed to be in His Heaven, and all was right in the world. On the evening of Saturday, 6 May 1837, Dickens and his wife took Mary to St James's Theatre and had an enjoyable evening. After returning home, and wishing each other good night, Dickens heard Mary cry out in pain. He ran to her bedroom, followed by his wife. The doctor was sent for. But she was beyond help. She died the following afternoon. He describes his grief in a letter to Mrs Hogarth:

> This was about 3 o'clock on the Sunday afternoon. They think her heart was diseased. It matters little to relate these details now, for the light and life of our happy circle is gone – and such a blank created as we can never supply.

The entire family was thunderstruck. Mary's mother was insensible for a week, Catherine and Charles were dumbfounded. To a friend he wrote a day after Mary died:

> You cannot conceive the misery in which this dreadful event has plunged us. Since our marriage she has been the peace and life of our home – the admired of all for her beauty and excellence – I could have better spared a much nearer relation or an older friend,

for she has been to us what we can never replace, and has left a blank which no one who ever knew her can have the faintest hope of seeing supplied.

To his very close friend, Tom Beard, he wrote: "Thank God she died in my arms and that the very last words she whispered were of me… I solemnly believe that so perfect a creature never breathed. I knew her inmost heart and her real worth and value. She had not a fault…" It seems that Dickens paid for the funeral and certainly intended to be buried in the same grave. He wrote the words for her tombstone: "Mary Scott Hogarth. Died 7th May 1837. Young, Beautiful and Good, God in His Mercy Numbered Her With His Angels at the Early Age of Seventeen." He wore her ring. In writing to Mary's mother, to thank her for sending him a lock of Mary Hogarth's hair, he said:

I have never had her ring off my finger by day or night, except for an instant at a time, to wash my hands, since she died. I have never had her sweetness and excellence absent from my mind so long. I can solemnly say that, waking or sleeping, I have never lost the recollection of our hard trial and sorrow, and I feel that I never shall… I wish you could know how I weary now for the three rooms in Furnival's Inn, and how I miss that pleasant smile and those sweet words which, bestowed upon our evening's work, in our merry banterings round the fire, were more precious to me than the applause of a whole world could be…

John Forster, who knew him well, recorded in his *Life of Charles Dickens* (1872) that Dickens' grief and suffering were intense, and affected him for years. His love for Mary would never diminish, he claimed to Forster. In May 1842, when he stood at Niagara Falls, he thought of Mary Scott Hogarth:

…what would I give if the dear girl whose ashes lie at Kensal Green had lived to come so far along with us – but she has been here many times… since her sweet face faded from my earthly sight.

On 25 October 1842, he wrote to Forster:

The desire to be buried next to her is as strong upon me now as it was five years ago; and I know (for I don't think there ever was love like that I bear her) that it will never diminish...

He told Forster he dreamed of her constantly and in 1844 he recounted a dream:

> ...I recognised the voice... I knew it was poor Mary's spirit. I was not at all afraid, but in great delight, so that I wept very much, and stretching out my arms to it as I called it 'Dear'...

In 1848 he wrote "This day eleven years, poor dear Mary died..." The memory, the dreams, never left him. As Forster recorded:

> With longer or shorter intervals this was with him all his days. Never from his waking thoughts was the recollection altogether absent; and though the dream would leave him for a time, it unfailingly came back... in the very year before he died, the influence was potently upon him. "She is so much in my thoughts at all times... that the recollection of her is an essential part of my being, and is as inseparable from my existence as the beating of my heart is..." Through later troubled years... whatever was worthiest in him found in this an ark of safety...

Dickens was deeply in love with his sister-in-law. She represented an angelic female perfection whose manifestation in human form was a miracle in his sight. Her loss was irreparable. He was completely unbalanced by her sudden death. He was forced to postpone writing the monthly parts of *Pickwick Papers* and *Oliver Twist*. Dickens felt an irresistible magnetism towards beautiful young women. This was to lead him into the arms of Ellen Ternan and create the idealized, innocent, saintly, young female figures – Rose Maylie, Little Nell, Florence Dombey, Agnes Wickfield, Esther Summerson and Amy Dorrit – which recur throughout his work.

There was reverse side to this coin. He was all too consciously aware of the sexual exploitation of women. His novels show that he was cognisant of the hidden side of Victorian sexuality – seduction, promiscuity and prostitution.

Later in his career he was to join forces with the philanthropist Angela Burdett-Coutts in rescuing prostitutes from a life of 'sin'. Miss Burdett-Coutts founded a residential home for the rehabilitation of street girls, where they were prepared for a new life in Australia.

Prostitution, endemic in London, Dickens had found deeply shocking since he got to know the ins and outs of this great, sprawling city. The Commissioner of Police deposed to the Society for the Suppression of Vice that in London there were 7,000 prostitutes, 933 brothels and 848 other 'disreputable houses' – the tone of his evidence was that his officers were doing a good job in suppressing vice. Other sources suggest this was a conservative estimate. Dickens' fiction is full of the terrors of the vice trade – from Nancy in *Oliver Twist* onwards – not always obvious to modern readers, but the clues are there. Mrs Nickleby learns that wicked Uncle Ralph proposes to have her young daughter Kate employed with a milliner and dress-maker, saying:

> Dress-makers in London, as I need not remind you, ma'am, who are so well acquainted with all matters in the ordinary routine of life, make large fortunes, keep equipages, and become persons of great wealth and fortune...

Mrs Nickleby is too unworldly to realise that 'milliner' was more or less an euphemism for prostitute. Many seamstresses took to prostitution as a means of supporting themselves. Dress-makers' shops were notorious as pick-up places for prostitutes and their clients. Readers of *Nicholas Nickleby* in the late 1830s would comprehend the hints from the descriptions of Madame Mantalini's premises, and the behaviour of Sir Mulberry Hawk. In *Dombey and Son* Dickens attempted analogously to portray the parallels between arranged society marriages (Mr Dombey and Edith Granger) and prostitution (Alice, Edith's first cousin, and Carker, Mr Dombey's business partner). In *David Copperfield*, Little Em'ly, Dan'l Peggoty's pathetic orphaned niece, is employed as a seamstress. She is seduced by Steerforth, David's school-friend, who takes her abroad and abandons her to the temptations of the vice trade. Her friend, Martha, is also a seamstress and prostitute. Ham says of her: "It's a poor wurem... as is trod underfoot by all the town. Up street and down street. The mould o' the churchyard don't hold any that the folk shrink away from, more..." Both Em'ly and Martha serve as models of the kind of redemption Dickens and Miss Coutts hoped for – they repent, and emigrate to Australia. Dickens was active in his support for Miss Coutts' efforts for about twelve years. This is a curious aspect of Dickens' life, which has yet properly to be examined.

It is almost certain that Dickens himself was a somewhat guilty client of working girls anxious to humanise what is, after all, an exploitative trade. The evidence for this is not wholly circumstantial. When he finally moved his family from Tavistock Place to Gad's Hill in September 1860 he had a major turn out of his correspondence. There was a large bonfire in which nearly all the letters from his friends were burned. We shall obviously never know what interesting evidence these might have contained, but from the hints which remain in letters which have survived, as well as some mysterious but nevertheless revealing clues in his behaviour recorded in evidence elsewhere and from what can be inferred, it is certain that Dickens had an adventurous and varied sex life from the days of his adolescence. He writes knowingly of the demi-monde in his fiction, and young females fall to preying males in *Nicholas Nickleby, Dombey and Son, David Copperfield.* He knows all about the customs and usages of the traffic in which young seamstresses supplemented their income, and when, where and how they were to be picked up. He has come down to us an advocate of family values, loving marriage partnerships, purity and sound morals, but all the evidence suggests that his days as a young man about town involved far more than going to places of public entertainment and hostelries. In one letter which has survived we learn that in 1841 he wrote to Daniel Maclise, attempting to entice him on a trip to Margate, offering as bait the fact that: " …there are conveniences of all kinds at Margate (do you take me?) and I know where they live." Much evidence is now coming to life to suggest that – like Thackeray, and Wilkie Collins – Dickens was a consistent sexual adventurer. His first major biographer, his friend John Forster, suppressed much, and Dickens tried to burn all links with the past when he made his bonfire of his letters from Macready, Ainsworth, Forster, Maclise, Lytton, and many others. (He asked his friends to destroy his letters to them, but fortunately none of them obliged). His young children remembered having "roasted onions in the ashes of the great." Dickens himself said that he wished "every letter I had ever written was on that pile" but many of his letters survived, and some of them are very interesting as evidence in this respect. Forster cut all references to Wilkie Collins in his *Life of Dickens*, and the omission may be significant – Collins lived a full and vigorous sex life, having notoriously been seduced in Italy at the age of thirteen by a married woman three times his age. This story he recounted with relish to Dickens, and they were frequent visitors to Paris to savour what Dickens called the 'diableries' together after they became friends and associates in the early 1850s. He spoke French well and although his accent was not perfect, he was voluble. He had been fascinated by France and French life since his thirties, and often made the trip with bachelor friends. As he wrote to his Swiss friend, William de Cerjat, in October 1864:

> ...my being on the Dover line, and my being very fond of France, occasion me to cross the channel perpetually... away I go by the mail-train, and turn up in Paris or anywhere else that suits my humour, next morning. So I come back as fresh as a daisy.

He claimed that these trips to France always did his neuralgia a power of good. His accounts of these trips seldom seem convincing. He may have been visiting Ellen Ternan there, or passing the time in other ways. He described them as solitary, "tours of observation" or "visiting a sick friend" or going for "a quiet tour" or to "evaporate for a fortnight" or even "a mysterious disappearance." After Dickens had left his wife for the young actress, Ellen Ternan, Wilkie Collins frequently twitted him about his being "as chaste as Diana" while on reading tours, which he ambiguously denied.

5   Dickens the performer

Towards the end of his professional life Dickens made an international reputation and a vast fortune as a public performer of his own work. These readings, as any who witnessed would testify, were a vent for his deep and powerful feelings and passions, of his vast range from comedy to pathos. He gave several tours of British cities and the USA.

These performances certainly exhausted him and probably hastened his death. During the final readings he was far from well. He was sleeping badly, was frequently faint, and suffered pain in his left eye and left foot.

He decided on his American Tour that when he returned he would give a series of Farewell Readings and then no more.

The Farewell Readings began in 1868. He prepared a special reading to enliven his performances at towns where he had read before. He told John Forster:

> I have made a short reading of the murder of Nancy in *Oliver Twist*. I cannot make up my mind, however, whether to do it or not. I have no doubt that I could petrify an audience by carrying out the notion I have of the way of rendering it. But whether the

impression would not be so horrible as to keep them away another time, is what I cannot satisfy myself upon. What do you think?

On 17 November 1868 it was presented to a specially invited audience of about a hundred at the St James' Hall. They saw Sikes round on Nancy, they saw him rain blows down on her helpless body, they saw her bloodstained face upturned begging for mercy. They were overwhelmed. A physician among the audience told him: "My dear Dickens, you may rely upon it that if only one woman cries out when you murder the girl, there will be a contagious of hysteria all over this place." A well known critic said that he thought the murder was the most amazing thing he had seen but that he had an almost irrepressible impulse to scream and if anyone had cried out, he, too would have followed.

The reading tour recommenced with the Sikes and Nancy murder in 1869 but was curtailed due to Dickens' failing health. They resumed in 1870.

Edmund Yates saw him read at St James's Hall on 27 February 1870 and wrote this account in *Tinsley's Magazine*:

> Gradually warming with excitement he flung aside his book and acted the scene of the murder, shrieked the terrified pleadings of the girl, growled the brutal savagery of the murderer, brought looks, tones, gestures simultaneously into play to illustrate his meaning, and there was not one of those who had known him best or who believed in him most, but was astonished at the power and versatility of his genius… It is here of course that the excitement of the audience is wrought up to its highest pitch, and that the acme of the actor's art is reached. The raised hands, the bent-back head, are good; but shut your eyes and the illusion is more complete. Then the cries for mercy, the 'Bill! dear Bill! for dear God's sake!' uttered in tones which the agony of fear prevails over the earnestness of the prayer, the dead, dull voice as hope departs, are intensely real. When the pleading ceases, you open your eyes in relief, in time to see the impersonation of the murderer seizing a heavy club and striking his victim to the ground.

His final reading on 15 March 1870 was attended by over two thousand and thirty people, and three times that number were turned away at the doors of the hall. As he strode on the platform at 8 o'clock exactly, the entire audience rose as one and cheered him to the echo. He had chosen to end his career with excerpts from *Carol* and *Pickwick*. An eye-witness attests that ill though he might have been, at this last performance he was at the peak of abilities:

> Not a point was lost. Every good thing told to the echo, that is through the echoing laughter. Scrooge, Fezziwig, the Fiddler, Topper, every one of the Cratchits, everybody in 'The Carol'... were all welcomed in turn, as became them, with better than acclamations. It was the same exactly with 'The Trial from Pickwick' – Justice Stareleigh, Serjeant Buzfuz, Mr Winkle, Mrs Cluppins, Sam Weller, one after another appearing for a brief interval, and then disappearing forever, each of them a delightfully humorous – one of them in particular, the Judge – a simply incomparable impersonation.
>
> Charles Kent: *Charles Dickens as a Reader*, 1872

At the end of the reading the applause was deafening – everyone stood. He returned to the platform and suddenly a great silence fell. He said:

> ...It would be worse than idle – for it would be hypocritical and unfeeling – if I were to disguise that I close this episode in my life with feelings of very considerable pain. For some fifteen years, in this hall and in many kindred places, I have had the honour of presenting my own cherished ideas before you for your recognition; and, in closely observing your reception of them, have enjoyed an amount of artistic delight and instruction which, perhaps, is given to few men to know...

He told them that he had always been grateful for the warm support of his public, but it was best to retire at the full flood tide of their favour. But, referring to the serialisation of *Drood*, he reminded them:

> ...in but two short weeks from this time I hope that you may enter, in your own homes, on a new series of readings, at which my assistance will be indispensable; but from these garish lights I vanish now forever more, with a heartfelt, grateful, respectful, and affectionate farewell.

At the end he was able to realise a lifelong ambition, to be a great performer. But he was also revealing what was basic in his method of composition – acting out in front of an audience the characters of his work as he was wont to do in front of a mirror at home, when he created them. Dickens characters are said to be caricatures: this is not quite right – they are dramatic creations who find themselves in narrative prose fiction, larger than life, but no less true.

DICKENS' ACHIEVEMENT:
analysis of the work

We have one great novelist who is gifted with the utmost power of rendering the external traits of our town population; and if he could give us their psychological character – their conceptions of life, and their emotions – with the same truth as their idiom and manners, his books would be the greatest contribution Art has ever made to the awakening of social sympathies. But while he can copy Mrs Plornish's colloquial style with the delicate accuracy of a sun-picture... he scarcely ever passes from the humorous and external to the emotional and tragic, without becoming as transcendental in his unreality as he was a moment before in his artistic truthfulness...

George Eliot: 'The Natural History of German Life',
Westminster Review, July 1856

...If the unconscious is the layer of experience which lies beneath the skin of rationality, then all Dickens' novels are, for better or worse, unconsciously repetitive. They are recapitulations and transformations of personal experience. The basic stuff may be exploited in many ways – symbolised, condensed, split, reconstituted; what is comic in one novel may surface as tragic in another. But for a writer in whom the autobiographical impulse is so strong and the sources of fiction so personal, all writing is to some extent 'unconscious repetition'. This is not to minimise Dickens' achievement. It is the reader's great delight to watch the combination and permutation of a limited stock of root notions into a variety that does not wither...

Elihu Pearlman: 'Inversion in *Great Expectations*' in Robert B.
Partlow, Jr, Editor: *Dickens Studies Annual*, Vol 7, Southern
Illinois UP, Carbondale and Edwardsville, 1978

In every respect, Dickens' achievement is special. He is certainly the most widely read major novelist in English and is widely read in translation. But more than that, and yet also part of that, is the fact that his work is integral to and enlivens English speaking culture. His characters are recognisable even by those who have not had an academic education. *A Christmas Carol* has become inextricably mixed up with the folklore of Christmas. His name exists adjectivally in the English language. Yet, just as his reputation is still constructing, so his identity in culture is still in the process of being constructed. Every film, television dramatisation etc of a Dickens novel, every stage performance or musical version serves further to adjust the full identity and nature of Charles Dickens.

There is another aspect to this. It is not enough to say that he has become "part of our popular culture" – the fact is that because of developing literacy, reading habits and the impact of printing technology and transport on methods of cultural production and consumption he was able to take root, thrive and grow as a creative artist, public figure and performer within a particularly vigorous stage of cultural development.

1　Early work

We do not know if Dickens was one of those who always wanted to write, but from the evidence we may surmise writing came naturally to him. He began work as a journalist when he was seventeen, taking short-hand notes at the courts at Doctors' Commons. From this he progressed to political reporting for *The True Sun, The Mirror of Parliament* and eventually *The Morning Chronicle*. From the beginning the voice is unmistakable. Here he is writing a report on the reception given in Edinburgh for Earl Grey. His Lordship was late, and one guest was so overcome by the tempting fare that he decided to tuck in before the competition arrived:

> ...He accordingly laid about him with right good-will. The example was contagious, and the clatter of knives and forks became general. Here upon, several gentlemen who were not hungry cried: "Shame!" too, eating nevertheless, all the while, as fast as they possibly could. In this dilemma, one of the stewards mounted a bench and feelingly represented to the delinquents the enormity of their conduct, imploring them, for decency's sake, to defer the process of mastication until the arrival of Earl Grey. This address was loudly cheered, but totally unheeded...
> *The Morning Chronicle*, 18 September 1834

The *Sketches by Boz*
The sharp observation, comicality, vitality and absurdity are characteristic. These qualities, in addition to a sense of melodrama and pathos, inform the *Sketches by Boz*, which is the title given to the two volume collection of his earliest published writings – descriptive journalism, fictional

portraits and stories – which came out in book form in 1836. These pieces first appeared in the *Monthly Magazine, Morning Chronicle* and *Bell's Life* in London.

The publishing history of the *Sketches* is fairly complicated but very interesting in what it reveals of Dickens' early career, and the value placed on his work by commercial publishers. The first series, called *Sketches by Boz, Illustrative of Every-day Life and Every-day People*, was published in two volumes by John Macrone, St James's Square, in 1836. Dickens wrote a Preface for this publication which, in the light of his subsequent literary success, seems extraordinarily prescient:

> In humble imitation of a prudent course, universally adopted by aeronauts, the Author of these volumes throws them up as his pilot balloon, trusting it may catch some favourable current, and was devoutly and earnestly hoping it may go off well...
>
> Unlike the generality of pilot balloons which carry no car, in this one it is very possible for a man to embark, not only himself, but all his hopes of future fame, and all his chance of future success... he can only entreat the kindness and favour of the public: his object has been to present little pictures of life and manners as they really are; and should they be approved of, he hopes to repeat his experiment with increased confidence, and on a more extensive scale.

This proved to be the case: in the meantime Dickens hit the jackpot with *Pickwick Papers*, serialised by Chapman and Hall from 31 March 1836. The sensational success of these monthly parts continued until October 1837.

The *Sketches by Boz* were conceived very much in the tradition of essayists such as Addison, Steele, Goldsmith, Lamb (whom Dickens in particular, greatly admired), Hazlitt and Leigh Hunt – are arranged under headings: 'Our Parish', 'Scenes' , 'Characters' and 'Tales'. They continue to be impressive at several levels. They are full of observation, drollery and pathos. They are vividly descriptive of London life of the period and have, in consequence, considerable historical interest. They are not without intrinsic literary merit, foreshadowing Dickens' later development. The observation is acute, the comicality characteristic, and the pathos frequently (and typically) excessive. The tensions and insecurities in the everyday life of the metropolitan bourgeoisie are convincingly explored.

'Our Parish' contains some character portraits – the Beadle,

Schoolmaster, Curate, Half-Pay Captain etc. – very much in the tradition of Theophrastus, Sir Thomas Overbury and *The Spectator's* Roger de Coverley stories. Many of the descriptive essays of sights, recreations, streets, institutions of the day – Doctors' Commons, Astley's Theatre, Gin-Shops, Vauxhall Gardens, Newgate – are evidence of his journalistic ability. He had a shrewd eye for detail and an interest in the underside of society, human oddity and cruelty amid the blandishments of civilisation. The sketches grouped under 'Characters' show the social interaction of some well observed character types. The revelation of desperate social pretension as a characteristic of urban life is typical of Dickens:

> ...only men are shabby-genteel; a woman is always either dirty and slovenly in the extreme, or neat and respectable, however poverty-stricken... A very poor man, 'who has seen better days'... is a strange compound of dirty-slovenliness and wretched attempts at faded smartness.
>
> 'Shabby-Genteel People'

The account of two clerks' roisterings ('Making a Night of It') rings true and is largely autobiographical. The Prisoner's Van is an account of the contents of the vehicle delivering social unfortunates from police stations to their various prison destinations. It contains the seeds of much of Dickens' later fictions – thieves, young prostitutes, vagrants, drunks and "boys of ten, as hardened in their vice as men of fifty."

'The Tales' show the novelist's powers in embryo. In particular a mannerism which was to be characteristic for the rest of his career – presenting a character by means of a vivid preliminary sketch, usually with a selection of relevant details, highlighting several idiosyncrasies by way of establishing an easily recognisable identity for every subsequent appearance:

> ...Septimus Hicks... was a tallish, white-faced young man, with spectacles, and a black ribbon round his neck instead of a neckerchief – a most interesting person; a poetical walker of the hospitals, and a "very talented young man." He was fond of lugging into the conversation all sorts of quotations from Don Juan, without fretting himself by the propriety of their application...

A fellow lodger remarks on a number of parcels seen in the hall. This is a cue for Hicks:

Materials for the toilet, no doubt...

– Much linen, lace, and several pair
Of stockings, slippers, brushes, combs, complete;
With other articles of ladies' fair,
To keep them beautiful, or leave them neat.

The other lodger asks if that is from Milton, to receive the reply: "No – from Byron" delivered with a look of profound contempt. ('The Boarding House').

These pieces are full of remarkable pre-echoes – preliminary drafts of Bumble, Mrs Rouncewell, the Artful Dodger, Bill Sikes, Montagu Tigg, Mrs Gamp. 'The Tuggs's at Ramsgate' is a searing exposure of the working actualities of snobbery, quite extraordinary from such a young writer. The leading Dickensian theme of the person respected in society, with some dark secret to hide, (paralleled in his case by the buried blacking factory episode) is comically bodied forth in the tale, Horatio Sparkins, the draper's assistant with social aspirations, who makes a great impression in society:

...Who could he be? He was evidently reserved, and apparently melancholy. Was he a clergyman? – he danced too well. A barrister? – he was not called. He used very fine words, and said a great deal. Could he be a distinguished foreigner come to England for the purpose of describing the country, its manners and customs; and frequenting public balls and public dinners... No, he had not a foreign accent. Was he a surgeon, a contributor to the magazines, a writer of fashionable novels, or an artist?...

But who is ultimately revealed to the young ladies he so hoped to impress, as plain Mr Samuel Smith: "the assistant at a cheap shop; the junior partner in a slippery firm of some three weeks' existence..."

The prose is certainly the most impressive feature of these stories. There is a fluidity, elegance, exactitude, cadence and expressiveness which seems to come naturally to him. He takes from language what is there, bends it to his uses, speaks with a voice wholly and unmistakably his own and he communicates a sense of relish and fun in using language. 'A

Passage in the Life of Watkins Tottle' has a theme he is to use several times – that of the man of considerable amorous ambition, oblivious of his formidable lack of attraction for the opposite sex:

> ...He was about fifty years of age; stood four feet six inches and three-quarters in his socks – for he never stood in stockings at all – plump, clean and rosy. He looked something like a vignette to one of Richardson's novels, and had a clean-cravatish formality of manner, and kitchen-pokerness of carriage, which Sir Charles Grandison himself might have envied...

There is a firm grasp of the tricks of melodrama – 'The Black Veil' tells the story of a surgeon persuaded by a woman to treat a dying man, who is confronted with the corpse of an executed criminal – the demented lady's own son. There is also in evidence that characteristic simultaneous combination of comicality and melodrama. 'Watkins Tottle' is a story of thwarted love which ends with Tottle drowning himself, yet it is told comically. This is clearly the same mind at work which was to create the immortal comic villain, Ebeneezer Scrooge.

The *Sketches by Boz* is a sampler of Dickens' range as an author, but this collection by no means prepared the world for the comic masterpiece which followed it – *The Posthumous Papers of the Pickwick Club*.

2   Pickwick Papers

The newly formed publishing firm of Chapman and Hall was seeking to commission a writer for an illustrated novel they intended to publish in monthly serial parts. They had followed Dickens' literary success with interest, and in fact had commissioned him to write 'The Tuggs of Ramsgate' for their *Library of Fiction* – a monthly periodical. They were attracted by the commercial success of *Sketches by Boz* and negotiated with the young writer.

The idea of *Pickwick Papers* is simplicity itself. Its rambling but entertaining structure and bold characterisation owes much to Dickens' early reading of Fielding and Smollett. The storyline is supposed to recount the travels around the country of the Pickwick Club, a comic equivalent to the new and much publicised British Association for the Advancement of Science. Pickwick himself was based on John Foster, a well-known fat old beau, of Richmond.

The novel opens at a London meeting of the Club, under its president, Samuel Pickwick. He sets out on a fact-finding tour of observation of scientific and cultural matters. He is accompanied by Nathaniel Winkle, a would-be sportsman, Augustus Snodgrass, a latter-day Byron, and Tracy Tupman, a plump but amorous bachelor. They travel first to Rochester, Stroud, Chatham and Brompton. The early writing is very much in the manner of the *Sketches by Boz*.

The first adventure happens in Rochester, where Winkle gets involved in a duel in a confusion of identities with Alfred Jingle, a strolling actor and con-man, who is one of Dickens' singular creations. Jingle is an excellent example of Dickens' basic style of character creation. We are given a vivid sketch of his appearance:

> ...about the middle height, but the thinness of his body, and the length of his legs, gave him the appearance of being much taller. The green coat had been a smart dress garment in the days of swallow-tails, but had evidently in those times adorned a much shorter man... for the soiled and faded sleeves scarcely reached to his wrists. It was buttoned closely up to his chin, at the imminent hazard of splitting the back; and an old stock, without a vestige of shirt collar, ornamented his neck. His scanty black trousers displayed here and there those shiny patches which bespeak long service, and were strapped very tightly over a pair of patched and mended shoes, as if to conceal the dirty white stockings, which were nevertheless visible. His long black hair escaped in negligent waves from beneath each side of his pinched-up hat, and glimpses of his bare wrists might be observed between the tops of his gloves and the cuffs of his coat sleeves. His face was thin and haggard; but an indescribable air of jaunty impudence and perfect self-possession pervaded the whole man...

He is not described again, as there is no need. He is brought to mind at every appearance the moment he begins to speak, as characteristically he is given an utterance uniquely his – something between verbal shorthand and abbreviated English used for brevity in telegrams, which Dickens describes as broken sentences "delivered with extraordinary volubility". This is Alfred Jingle's characteristic description of the tourist attractions of Rochester:

Ah! fine place... glorious pile – frowning walls – tottering arches
– dark nooks – crumbling staircases – Old cathedral too – earthy
smell – pilgrims' feet worn away the old steps – little Saxon doors
– confessionals like money-takers' boxes at theatres – queer
customers these monks – Popes, and Lord Treasurers, and all
sorts of fellows, with great red faces, and broken noses, turning
up every day – buff jerkins too – matchlocks – Sarcophagus –
fine place – old legends too – strange stories: capital...

The technique is simple but effective: the character is developed
through speech, and once developed is instantly recognisable. The effect
in Jingle is extremely comic. As Dickens' art matures and his satiric and
social themes become more serious, the technique is refined to suit his
purpose. But nevertheless Micawber, Gradgrind, Joe Gargery, Jaggers,
Podsnap and other figures are created on this model.

There are other qualities to note in the writing of *Pickwick Papers*.
The novelist consciously develops the comic potential of his prose itself,
strikingly so, for there are numerous moments in this novel which are
funny, not so much for the incidents narrated, but for the very way in
which they are written. The comedy is in the prose, or to put it another
way, the prose is comic. Here is an account of the effects of a good dinner
and an ample sufficiency of wine on Samuel Pickwick:

...That gentleman had gradually passed through the various stages
which precede the lethargy produced by dinner, and its
consequences. He had undergone the ordinary transitions from
the height of conviviality to the depth of misery, and from the
depth of misery to the height of conviviality. Like a gas lamp in
the street, with the wind in the pipe, he had exhibited for a moment
an unnatural brilliancy; then sunk so low as to be scarcely
discernible: after a short interval he had burst out again, to
enlighten for a moment, then flickered with an uncertain,
staggering sort of light, and then gone out altogether...

The scene, in itself, is nothing. Its depiction is everything. *Pickwick
Papers* is packed with such writing. It is as if the writer had suddenly
tapped a vast reservoir of comicality, stored in his person for this moment.
All the evidence suggests Dickens' ability to generate wonderful copy
off the hoof, from day to day observations, social gossip, fragments from
his own youthful reading and inspirations from his daily work as a

journalist. Sam Weller, probably initially intended as a minor comic character was based on the renowned Cockney comedian, Simon Vale, who had notably performed the role of Simon Spatterdash in Samuel Beazley's farce *Boarding House* at the Surrey Theatre in 1822. Spatterdash had earned his laughs largely by his stage-Cockney patter on the "as the so-and-so said as he etc. etc." model, which Dickens developed as Sam Weller's major means of utterance: "Business first, pleasure arterwards, as King Richard the Third said, when he stabbed the t'other king in the Tower, afore he smothered the babbies..."

The character of Sam Weller made *Pickwick Papers* successful. Dickens also worked in material about his father, in the shape of Tony Weller, ("a rayther stout gen'l'm'n of eight-and-fifty") with his marital problems. The Jingle duel farce is almost certainly based on recollections from Sheridan's *The Rivals*. The Pickwick and Sam Weller relationship, clearly parallels Don Quixote and Sancho Panza (as was noted by contemporaries) and Dickens may have been inspired by Smollett's *Sir Lancelot Greaves*. This gives Dickens the opportunity, which he seized upon, to provide contrasting views of reality – Pickwick's naïve childish-foolish optimism and Weller's scepticism. The Bardell-Pickwick trial, one of the great set pieces of the novel, in which poor old Pickwick is sued for breach of promise, after his intention to hire a manservant is deliberately misconstrued by the widow Bardell, was based on the infamous Melbourne-Norton trial. Pickwick loses the case, during which Sam Weller is a star witness. Dickens had reported on these court proceedings, in which George Norton cited the Prime Minister, Lord Melbourne, for criminal connection with his wife, Lady Caroline Norton, held under Sir Stephen Gazelee (whom Dickens transforms into Stareleigh). The prosecution was vigorously conducted by Serjeant Bompas (who becomes Serjeant Buzfuz) and the novelist actually parodies the slender documentary evidence brought forth by the prosecuting counsel.

Other key episodes are the Eatanswill election, which portrays the conduct of representative parliamentary democracy in the early 1830s, and visits to Bristol, Ipswich, Bath and the Kentish idyll at Dingley Dell. The novel is packed with comic episodes – the military review at Chatham, Pickwick's curious adventures at a girls' boarding school, Winkle's wooing of Arabella Allen, and Tony Weller's final showdown with his rival, the Revd. Stiggins. The climax of *Pickwick Papers* is Mr Pickwick's imprisonment in the Fleet at his refusal to pay Mrs Bardell's damages. Here he meets Mrs Bardell, who has been sent there for non-payment of her legal costs. Pickwick agrees to pay her debts on condition she waives all claims on him. Jingle makes a fresh start in Australia. The Club is wound up. Sam Weller marries a pretty maidservant and Pickwick retires to a cosy dwelling in Dulwich, taking Sam and his wife with him as his servants.

Pickwick Papers is a quintessentially English masterpiece, yet simultaneously universal, enshrining as it does a last, wholesome glimpse of all that was best in the world before the mad headlong dash into global industrialism and mass consumerism:

> As the coach rolls swiftly past the fields and orchards, which skirt the road, groups of women and children, piling the fruit in the sieves, or gathering the scattered ears of corn, pause for an instant from their labour, and shading the sun-burnt face with a still browner hand... gaze upon the passengers with curious eyes, while some stout urchin, too small to work, but too mischievous to be left at home, scrambles over the side of the basket in which he has been deposited for security, and kicks and screams with delight. The reaper stops in his work, and stands with folded arms, looking at the vehicle as it whirls past... You cast a look behind you, as you turn a corner of the road...
>
> Chapter 16

He was in his mid twenties as he wrote *Pickwick*, and we can see how rapidly his art was developing. For the plot outline he takes over the kind of narrative exploited by Smollett, the story of a pair of characters, a master and servant figure, retelling their adventures as they travel the country. But instead of a *picaresque* story, retailing the story of a rogue, we have the benign Pickwick and his shrewd valet. The early chapters contain rather laboured jokes, a lack of direction and some contrived action highlights. The interpolated tales, possibly previously written unpublished oddments, are irrelevant and tedious. But once Jingle and Sam Weller have established themselves, the story gathers pace. He lavishes his comic invention on the most extraordinarily well observed details of behaviour – Sam Weller settling down to write a love letter:

> ...looking carefully at the pen to see that there were no hairs in it, and dusting down the table, so that there should be no crumbs

of bread under the paper, Sam tucked up the cuffs of his coat, squared his elbows, and composed himself to write...

Or Pickwick's predicament as he attempts to regain his hat, lost in the wind:

> There are very few moments in a man's existence when he experiences so much ludicrous distress, or meets with so little charitable commiseration, as wherein he is in pursuit of his own hat. A vast deal of coolness, and a peculiar degree of judgement, are requisite in catching a hat. A man must not be precipitate, or he runs over it; he must not rush into the opposite extreme, or he loses it altogether. The best way is, to keep gently up with the object of pursuit, to be wary and cautious, to watch your opportunity well, get gradually before it, then make a rapid dive, seize it by the crown, and stick it firmly on your head: smiling pleasantly all the time, as if you thought it as good a joke as anybody else.

Pickwick Papers was a publishing triumph in spite of its initially sluggish sales. It became a craze and brought much merchandise in its wake – there were Pickwick hats, canes, walking-sticks, song-books, joke-books, writing-paper, cigars, toasting-forks. In today's hype, the merchandise precedes the media event. Everybody read it – physicians between patients, judges while juries were out. It was read aloud to gatherings and groups at work and at home. One reader broke a blood-vessel laughing at it. A mortally sick man, told he had but a month to live, rejoiced he would live to read at least one further monthly number. It is a landmark in book publishing. Chapman and Hall decided to issue it cloth bound as a single volume after its completion in 1837, with the title in gold lettering instead of paper labels. Thus the novel led the way, with innovations in quality of paper, illustrations and general production which were to become standard in publishing. Dickens himself declared:

> If I were to live a hundred years, and write three novels in each, I should never be so proud of any of them, as I am of Pickwick, feeling as I do, that it has made its own way, and hoping, as I own I do hope, that long after my hand is withered as the pens it held, Pickwick will be found on many a dusty shelf with many a better work...

This novel was scarcely properly underway, the fifth number was on the bookstalls, when Dickens was contracted by Richard Bentley to edit his new monthly magazine, *Bentley's Miscellany*. He also agreed to write a novel to be serialised from 31 January 1837. This was *Oliver Twist*.

3 *Oliver Twist*

This novel continues and develops Dickens' mastery of narrative prose melodrama, combining as it does several quite standard ingredients of the day – a pregnant young woman abandoned by her lover, an orphan (the dispossessed heir) thrown upon the world, irredeemable villains, a few saints, murder, death-bed confession and amazing reversals of fortune.

The plot mechanism is fairly simple. An unprincipled young man, already married with a son, courts his wife's sister, Agnes, and promises to marry her. She becomes pregnant. The young man dies. In his will he leaves the bulk of his estate to Agnes's child, provided he retain an unblemished character. Agnes, in very reduced circumstances, seeks relief in the workhouse, where she dies in childbirth. The son is named Oliver Twist and is handed over to the local workhouse orphanage. At the age of nine Oliver enters the workhouse to suffer, starve and earn his keep with other boys picking oakum. He is selected spokesman for his companions and asks for more gruel. Bumble the Beadle then apprentices him to the local undertaker, where after enduring much torment, he runs away to London. Here he is picked up by the Artful Dodger, one of old Fagin's star pupils in the art of pickpocketing, and is apprenticed to a life of thieving.

He is arrested after a bungled attempt at robbing a man in a bookstall but is taken under the wing of the good Mr Brownlow, who had observed the incident. Brownlow has him nursed back to health in his house in Pentonville, then a fashionable suburb in North London. Oliver is regarded as a danger to Fagin's gang, as he knows too much about their activities. Bill Sikes, a vicious burglar, under Fagin's orders, takes Oliver under his wing with the help of Nancy, his mistress, and they use Oliver to break into Mrs Maylie's house at Chertsey. The job is bungled, Sikes escapes but Oliver is wounded in the arm. Mrs Maylie and her adopted niece look after him.

Oliver tells them his history. The villains have Oliver watched by the evil prowling Monks, who is one of Fagin's agents. They now plot to regain Oliver. Nancy has been moved by Oliver's suffering and confides in Rose Maylie. Fagin learns of Nancy's betrayal and he tells Bill, who murders Nancy in one of Dickens' most brutal and dramatic scenes. Sikes flees from justice but falls from the rooftops and accidentally hangs himself. Fagin is tried and hanged and the gang broken up. Mr Brownlow adopts Oliver and has resolved the mystery of his birth and revealed that Oliver is Monks' half brother. According to the father's will, Oliver would inherit the paternal estate, provided he remain wholly virtuous and blameless. Monks goes to America with his share of the legacy, but dies in prison. Bumble and his wife, who were co-conspirators against Oliver, are themselves now confined to the workhouse.

Social themes
The enduring power of this novel is hardly to be found in any originality of plot or setting, which is very much of the 'Newgate Novel' school, then very much in vogue. *The Newgate Calendar*, or *The Malefactors' Bloody Register*, had been published since 1774 and contained biographies of the most notorious criminals and detailed their crimes. The taste for crime was continued in the so-called Newgate Novels which featured the lives, adventures and crimes of murderers, robbers, highwaymen, fences, thief-takers and the whole sordid glamour of the criminal underworld, which played up the violence, excitement and glamour of crime for popular appeal. Several of Dickens' contemporary novelists, including Harrison Ainsworth and Bulwer Lytton, successfully contributed to this craze for lurid crime fiction. Dickens exploited this genre for his own purposes which were mainly to highlight the hideous injustices of the social system, especially as hardship became institutionalised under the provisions of the Poor Law Amendment Act 1834. It was this Act which created the workhouse system to replace the previous system of outdoor poor-relief.

Workhouse uniform was worn. No pauper was allowed outside except with special permission. Smoking was forbidden. Husbands and wives were kept separately and children were separated from their parents. There were no books, not even bibles. Meals were eaten in silence. Parents had no right to see their own children in the same workhouse even once a day. The work offered was soul destroying and almost repellent – stone-breaking, oakum-picking, corn-grinding. If the sole aim was economic, then the new Poor Law was successful, for within three years the cost of poor relief was reduced by 36 percent, but the human cost was incalculable. The idle, indigent, paupers, vagrants, drunkards, prostitutes, old, infirm, crippled, ailing and foundling children were all thrown together. What enraged Dickens was the effect on children, who were stigmatised, probably for life, as workhouse brats. They received no education to speak of, exposed to all manner of evil influence and apprenticed by their workhouse guardians as soon as possible to get them off the rates.

In April 1841 Dickens, in writing a Preface for the third edition of *Oliver Twist*, had the opportunity to discuss his reasons for writing this novel, and he lays bare his moral intentions. He admits that the subject matter of the London Underworld may be shocking and coarse and the characters degraded, but he hoped to show

> the principle of Good surviving through every adverse circumstance, and triumphing at last

and that he was writing against the fashion of the Newgate Novel. He goes out of his way to attack to mode for criminals portrayed as:

> seductive fellows, amiable for the most part, faultless in dress, plump in pocket, choice in horseflesh, bold in bearing, fortunate in gallantry, great at a song, a bottle, pack of cards or dice-box, and fit companions for the bravest. But I had never met (except in Hogarth) with the miserable reality. It appeared to me that to draw a knot of such associates in crime as really do exist; to paint them in all their deformity, in all their wretchedness, in all the squalid poverty of their lives; to show them as they really are, forever skulking through the dirtiest paths of life, with the great, black, ghastly gallows closing up their prospect... it appeared to me that to do this, would be to attempt something which was greatly needed, and which would be a service to society...

In this Preface he brackets himself with Defoe, Fielding, Smollett and Goldsmith in attempting to portray such scenes with high moral intention. In this respect *Oliver Twist* is a major contribution to literature, and Dickens' letters and speeches further testify his opposition to the application of harsh Benthamite utilitarian principles to social institutions and to human beings.

This novel is significant in another respect. It introduces two important aspects of his art which are to remain constant – the child figure, and the lavish use of symbols, images, metaphors to give his narrative prose a poetic quality. *Oliver Twist* is an examination of the horrors of loneliness and alienation. We note the sadness Oliver feels when he leaves his little friends in the workhouse: "…they were the only friends he had ever known; and a sense of his loneliness in the great world sank into the child's heart for the first time…" It is significant that Oliver's punishment for asking for more was that he was made more lonely. He is confined to a dark and solitary room: "consigned by the wisdom and mercy of the board" and he cried all day, when

> the long dismal night came on (he) spread little hands before his eyes to shut out the darkness, and crouching in the corner, tried to sleep: ever and anon waking with a start and tremble, and drawing himself closer and closer to the wall, as if to feel its cold hard surface were a protection in the gloom and loneliness which surrounded him.

At the coffin-maker's his loneliness and isolation is stressed and when he runs away his "lonesomeness and desolation" are emphasised as he creeps into Barnet. Oliver had lamented his loneliness to Mr Bumble even before he was employed at the undertaker's. It is an elegant touch that Bumble's buttons display the image of the Good Samaritan.

Oliver's situation is accompanied by symbols of winter, desolation and death. As his fortunes change, under the guidance of his saviours, he seems to be given the sun once more – the significance of Rose's surname, Maylie, should not escape us. The villains of the piece, in contrast, exist in a gloomy and sunless atmosphere. Sikes is always found at night time, in public houses "where flaring gas-light burnt all day in the winter time: and where no ray of sun ever shone in the summer…" This is continued in the scene where Sikes tries to prevent the sun shining into the murder-room: "He tried to shut it out, but it would stream in…" Fagin is frequently presented in terms of night, slime, offal and so on. The theme of the battle between goodness, innocence, purity – and evil, corruption is a constant one in the novels, and Dickens frequently placed a child in a metropolis of cynical evil: "One needs to be sharp in this town, my dear… and that's the truth" Fagin says. This is endlessly recycled in his fiction. The unhappy and neglected child becomes for Dickens the image of injustice and the indictment of a materialistic society. With his own ineradicable memories of childhood suffering, it was naturally easy for him to write about such feelings of injustice. The child works as a double symbol, concerned with the child-in-the-family – a plea for unity and love in the natural domestic order – and also as symbol of modern man, lost in a world of his own making.

4   *Nicholas Nickleby*

For plot construction, Dickens resorts to his admired Smollett, and provides a series of adventures and miscellaneous incidents, simply held together by the fact that they happen consecutively to the leading characters, Nicholas and his sister Kate. These two young people are thrown penniless into life when their father dies. Their mother, a simple, well-meaning but scatterbrained lady (based on the novelist's mother) appeals for help to her late husband's brother, the melodramatic stage-villain, Ralph Nickleby. Ralph sneers at Mrs Nickleby's distress, mocking her husband's failure to make proper provision for his family. He takes a deep dislike to the hearty and open Nicholas, and grudgingly obtains for him the post of teaching assistant at a boys' boarding school in Yorkshire. Kate is offered an apprenticeship with Mrs Mantalini, who keeps a milliner's shop. The Yorkshire schools were notorious as the dumping ground for the illegitimate children of parents who wanted them kept well out of the way – at this time Yorkshire was well beyond easy travelling distance of the south of England and it was a useful way of keeping such indiscretions secret. The harsh living conditions, dreadful food, poor teaching and barbarous cruelty were widely rumoured. One notorious Yorkshire schoolmaster, William Shaw, was tried in 1823 for the gross neglect of boys in his charge. Kate, too, is being introduced to a seamy world, as milliners' shops were renowned breeding grounds for prostitution.

Dickens had been fascinated by the horrors of the Yorkshire schools since the day in his boyhood when another boy told him how he had been operated on with a penknife to extract an abscess. In January 1838 he travelled to Yorkshire with Hablot Browne (Phiz), his illustrator, to research Yorkshire schools. He told Forster he was resolved to attack the "Cheap Schools" in Yorkshire "to which public attention had been painfully drawn" by a recent law case "which had been notorious for cruelties committed in them, whereof he had heard as early as his childish days; and which he was bent upon destroying if he could."

Nicholas finds Dotheboys Hall a terrible place. The one-eyed headmaster, Wackford Squeers, is a monster, whose ignorance is deep and whose cruelty boundless. Nicholas is shocked and loses his control when, Smike, a poor drudge of a pupil, runs away and is captured and brought back in triumph for a public beating by Squeers. With a speech straight out of melodrama, Nicholas beats Squeers to within an inch of his life:

> Wretch... touch him at your peril! I will not stand by and see it done; my blood is up, and I have the strength of ten such men as you. Look to yourself, for by Heaven, I will not spare you, if you drive me on!... I have a long series of insults to avenge... and my indignation is aggravated by the dastardly cruelties practised on helpless infantry in this foul den...

Nicholas then flees to London, taking the unfortunate Smike with him. He is befriended by the strange, kindly, alcoholic Newman Noggs, who works as a clerk to Ralph Nickleby. Nicholas becomes tutor to the daughters of Mrs Kenwigs, one of Noggs's neighbours. Meanwhile Kate is suffering the advances of Mrs Mantalini's affected husband. Ralph tries to pass her off to one of his aristocratic associates. She is insulted at a dinner given by his friends, Lord Mulbury Hawk and Sir Frederick Verisopht. Ralph takes her away from the Mantalini establishment and sets her up as companion to the snobbish Mrs Wititterley.

Nicholas, having quarrelled with Ralph, joins the theatrical company of Vincent Crummles, as playwright and actor. Noggs informs him of Ralph's intrigues. He overhears a conversation between Hawk and Verisopht in which his sister's reputation is impugned and he gives Hawk a beating. Verisopht is later killed in duel by Hawk. Nicholas's fortunes improve when he meets the philanthropic Cheeryble brothers who employ him as a clerk and install the Nickleby family in a rural cottage in Bow. Nicholas falls in love with Madeline Bray, daughter of an ailing debtor, enmeshed by Ralph Nickleby. Ralph is conspiring to marry Madeline off to one Arthur Gride, who has in his possession a document which entails Madeline to a considerable property. She has unwittingly promised to marry him in exchange for his repaying her father's debts. On the morning of this connived marriage, Bray dies of a heart attack and it is discovered that Madeline is, in fact, heiress to a considerable fortune. Ralph is exposed as the father of Smike, who unfortunately dies, telling Nicholas on his death bed of his everlasting love for Kate Nickleby.

Ralph's crimes now overtake him and he hangs himself. Nicholas marries Madeline. Kate marries the Cheerybles' nephew, Frank. Squeers is transported to Australia and Dotheboys Hall is disbanded and: "began to be forgotten by the neighbours, or only to be spoken of as among the things that had been."

Nickleby is riddled with inconsistencies, though it contains some invigorating scenes and characteristic comedy. An anonymous contemporary review expresses this well:

> ...the hero himself has no character at all, being but the walking thread-paper to convey the various threads of the story. Kate is no better; and the best-drawn characters in the book, Mr Mantalini and Mrs Nickleby, have only caricature parts to play; and in preserving them, there is no great difficulty... Squeers and Ralph Nickleby become worse and worse as the story proceeds... Squeers at first is nothing more than an ignorant and wretched hound, making a livelihood for himself and his family by starving a miserable group of boys. The man has not the intellect for any thing better or worse; and yet we find at last an adept in disguising himself, in ferreting out hidden documents, in carrying through a difficult and entangled scheme of villainy. Ralph Nickleby makes his appearance as a shrewd, selfish, hard-hearted usurer, intent on nothing but making and hoarding money; in the end we find him actuated by some silly feelings of spite or revenge, by which he cannot... make a farthing... His committing suicide, and that out of remorse too, is perfectly out of character... (he) has not done anything that could expose him to legal inconvenience...
>
> *Fraser's Magazine*, April 1840

It has not achieved a high place in Dickens' works, but it requires to be read at its own level. We cannot bring to this work expectations of finding the subtlety of Henry James, the irony of Jane Austen, the moral complexities of George Eliot – but read as socially conscious melodrama, it emerges as very highly charged and full of striking moments and telling points. It has retained its popularity. The Yorkshire school scenes are memorable and several of the characters – Mrs Nickleby, the Mantalinis, Newman Noggs and the pathetic Smike – are among his immortal creations. Much of the descriptive prose strains to make its effects and even when read in context the moments of high drama seldom aspire much beyond stage melodrama. The moment of Verisopht's death, for example:

> The two shots were fired, as nearly as possible, at the same instant.
> In that instant, the young lord turned his head sharply round,

fixed upon his adversary a ghastly stare, and, without a groan or stagger, fell down dead.

Or Ralph Nickleby's unlikely dying words as a church bell is carried to him on the wind as he is about to hang himself:

> Lie on!... with your iron tongue! Ring merrily for the births that make expectants writhe, and for marriages that are made in hell, and toll ruefully for the dead whose shoes are worn already! Call men to prayers who are godly because not found out, and ring chimes for the coming in of every year that brings this cursed world nearer to its end. No bell or book for me! Throw me on a dunghill, and let me rot there, to infect the air!

Above all considerations, Dickens' ability to present character, simultaneously comic and grotesque, and in prose which is in itself comic, is once again demonstrable. Here is the masterly portrait of Wackford Squeers:

> He had but one eye, and the popular prejudice runs in favour of two. The eye he had, was unquestionably useful, but decidedly not ornamental; being of a greenish grey, and in shape resembling the fan-light of a street door. The blank side of his face was much wrinkled and puckered up, which gave him a very sinister appearance, especially when he smiled, at which times his expression bordered on the villainous. His hair was very flat and shiny, save at the ends, where it was brushed stiffly up from a low protruding forehead, which assorted well with his harsh voice and coarse manner. He was about two or three and fifty, and a trifle below the middle size; he wore a white neckerchief with long ends, and a suit of scholastic black; but the coat sleeves being a great deal too long, and his trousers a great deal too short, he appeared ill at ease in his clothes, and as if he were in a perpetual state of astonishment at finding himself so respectable...

5   *The Old Curiosity Shop*

Charles Dickens had always read and admired 18th century writers, not only the major novelists, but also the periodic journalists – Joseph Addison, Richard Steele, Oliver Goldsmith. He tried to imitate them in a new periodical – *Master Humphrey's Clock*, which he edited.

The best idea of the work, as he explained to John Forster, "might be given perhaps by reference to the *Tatler*, the *Spectator*, and Goldsmith's *Bee*; but it would be far more popular both in the subjects of which it treats and its mode of treating them." The plan was for a weekly publication containing papers from a club, rather in the manner of the *Sir Roger De Coverley* papers, containing new stories of established favourites such as Sam Weller, Pickwick, Tony Weller, as well as several new pieces of fiction. This miscellany would be held together by the character of old Master Humphrey, into the casement of whose splendid grandfather clock the various members of his circle deposited their manuscripts. Sales initially were good, but tailed off once the public realised that they were not being offered another, full length novel in serial form. But Dickens had begun *The Old Curiosity Shop*, the story of Little Nell, which took possession of his imagination and was serialised.

This may not be a better novel than *Nicholas Nickleby*, but it is unquestionably better Dickens. It shares with *Pickwick Papers* the undoubted mark of a unique literary personality. The plot outline is straightforward. Grandfather Trent runs an antique shop, full of old armour, quaint paintings, old furniture, which contrasts extraordinarily with the stunning beauty of his divine and innocent granddaughter, Nell. Nell's mother has died, and in his grief old Trent wishes Nell to be brought up as a lady. To fulfil this ambition he needs immense wealth, which he proposes to gain by gambling. This soon gets him into serious debt with the vicious dwarf, Daniel Quilp:

> An elderly man of remarkably hard features and forbidding aspect, and so low in stature as to be quite a dwarf, though his head and face were large enough for the body of a giant. His black eyes were restless, sly and cunning; his mouth and chin, bristly with the stubble of a coarse hard beard; and his complexion was one of that kind which never looks clean or wholesome. But what added most to the grotesque appearance of his face, was a ghastly smile, which appearing to be the mere result of habit and to have no connection with any mirthful or complacently feelings, constantly revealed the few discoloured fangs which were yet scattered in his mouth...

He pours boiling neat gin down his throat, crunches up eggs with their shells still on them, torments his wife and relatives to death – yet he has a magnetic sexual allure. Trent senses that Quilp has sexual designs on his beloved Nell, so to escape the financial clutches of Quilp and his conniving lawyer, Samson Brass, Trent and Nell flee London and travel to the Midlands. En route they meet Codlin and Short, travelling showmen with a classic Punch and Judy act, Mrs Jarley and her famous travelling waxworks, drunken bargees and a dedicated schoolmaster who offers them accommodation in a secluded village. The descriptions of the industrial landscape and turbulent city life are extremely vivid, and Dickens incorporates much contemporary material, including his own recent observations of the Black Country, as well as the Chartist agitations of the day. Roles are reversed, as Nell becomes a mother to old Trent. Tension is maintained by Nell's constant attempts to save old Trent from himself and keep him away from card-sharps, as well as the various attempts to track them down by villainous as well as good characters.

The lawyer's clerk, Dick Swiveller, begins to understand the nature of Quilp's operations, and tries to work against Brass and Quilp. Dick is a superb creation. He is given, when we first meet him, Dickens' usual colourful description by way of visiting card, but he expresses himself in the most superbly idiosyncratic utterance. It is a mixture of romantic poetical fragments, half remembered Shakespeare, seasoned with fragments of traditional and popular culture, which combines to create the most dazzling seedy-poetic expression – "…what is the odds so long as the fire of the soul is kindled at the taper of conwiviality, and the wing of friendship never moults a feather? What is the odds so long as the spirit is expanded by means of rosy wine, and the present moment is the least happiest of our existence?" He saves Kit Nubbles, who used to work for Trent, from Quilp's persecution. He makes friends with the Brass's hard-pressed servant girl, known as the Marchioness, who is in fact the illegitimate daughter of Quilp and Samson's formidable sister, Sally Brass. The Marchioness nurses Dick through a serious illness and they become inseparable in a memorable courtship in which he teaches her cribbage and much else about life – one of Dickens' supreme inventive sequences, enchantingly combining pathos and ludicrous elements. Their bliss is supported by a timely legacy from Dick's aunt. Kit Nubbles nobly supports his mother and family by working for the Garland family, and falls in love with their maid, Barbara.

Quilp's villainies are about to be exposed, but he is drowned in a melodramatic scene well worthy of his larger-than-life qualities. All the while a curious stranger has been making enquiries about Trent and Nell. He is Trent's brother, who has made a fortune in the Antipodes. He tracks them down, but he is too late. Nell has died from her long ordeal. Trent goes mad and dies on her grave. Samson Brass is imprisoned. Dick, having no idea of the origins of his beloved Marchioness, gives her the suitably mysterious name Sophronia Sphinx, and they are married. Kit and Barbara are married.

This novel has had a mixed press. Contemporary readers were gripped by it and wept copiously over the death of Little Nell. Modern readers are urged to cling to the 'best bits' – Dick, the Marchioness, Quilp – and dismiss the 'mawkish' Nell with Oscar Wilde's over cited dictum about having to have a heart of stone to read the death of Little Nell without laughing. Aesthetic evaluation of this novel is severely distorted, not so much by Wilde's remark as by the huge shift in taste which has occurred since the early Victorian period, which seems particularly to have affected literature. *The Old Curiosity Shop*, like any other work of art, must be taken whole. We need to explore what Dickens was trying to do, what kind of society did he see around him, what were his contemporaries reading in the newspapers at the time? This needs to be said. But while admitting that this novel is an unsatisfactory conflation of melodrama, pathos and fancy, the book is permeated by passionate outrage at the consequences of industrialism:

> ...strange engines spun and writhed like tormented creatures; clanking their chains... Men, women, children, wan in their looks and ragged in their attire, tended the engines... begged upon the road, or scowled half-naked from the doorless houses... But night time in this dreadful spot! – night, when the smoke was changed to fire... when bands of unemployed labourers paraded in the roads... when some called for bread, and some for drink to drown their cares; and some with tears, and some with staggering feet... went brooding home...
>
> *The Old Curiosity Shop*, Chapter 45

Published as thousands of the nation's population toiled, starved and suffered at the hands of an economy run on the principles of the casino, Dickens' novel bodies forth the story of a parent ruined by the gambler's urge and in the process destroying his dear child. Read properly in context, the death of Little Nell is in fact a very moving piece of writing:

> For she was dead. There, upon her little bed, she lay at rest. The solemn stillness was no marvel now.

She was dead. No sleep so beautiful and calm, so free from trace of pain, so fair to look upon. She seemed a creature fresh from the hand of God, and waiting for the breath of life; not one who had lived and suffered death...

6 *Barnaby Rudge*

Barnaby Rudge was long gestating in the novelist's imagination. Originally entitled *Gabriel Varden, the Locksmith of London*, it was contracted by Macrone, and should have been published at the end of 1836. Dickens wriggled out of his obligations to Macrone, and handed the rights to Bentley, and promised it for 1838. He found writing *Oliver Twist* and *Nicholas Nickleby* obviated the composition of *Barnaby*. Bentley eventually accepted £1,500 for his rights in *Oliver Twist* and the forthcoming *Barnaby Rudge*, and Dickens was able to deal solely with Chapman and Hall. The complexity of these contractual arrangements is matched by the complexity of the novel's origins in the Dickens' imagination.

He had been turning the subject over in his mind for five years. Several strands come together. He had always been obsessed with the great central image of Newgate prison – "this gloomy depository of the guilt and misery of London" – as he described it in 'A Visit to Newgate' (*Sketches by Boz*). He intended to stand Newgate as a massive presence and a symbol. He clearly wanted to attempt a vast historical novel in the manner of Sir Walter Scott, and continuously found the behaviour of mobs and crowds fascinating (this resurfaces in *A Tale of Two Cities*, and Charles Mackay's *Popular Delusions and the Behaviour of Crowds* (1845) was in his library at Gad's Hill). He selected the subject of the Gordon Riots of 1780 quite early, being particularly taken with the terrible rumour that the rioters had released the mentally ill and psychotic from Bedlam.

The central moment in the novel was originally to be Gabriel Varden, the brave locksmith, barring the rampaging mob from entering Newgate, producing scenes paralleled to Scott's dramatic account of the storming of the Tolbooth during the Porteus Riots in 1736 in *The Heart of Midlothian* (1818). Gradually his plans changed, possibly as a result of the impact on his imagination of Thomas Carlyle's *History of the French Revolution*, published in 1837. Dickens read this work constantly, and carried it in his pocket. He heard Carlyle lecture in 1840 and was deeply impressed. Dickens became far more involved with the motivation and behaviour of the crowd, than just with the sturdy and heroic figure of Gabriel Varden. As the economy so seriously deteriorated, the Chartist challenge became more pressing and public order became such an issue, Dickens found the manifestation of the mob an ever more suitable subject. In 1839 there were Chartist riots in Birmingham during July and at Newport in November. Dickens was a young reporter in the gallery at the Commons when one of the most dreadful political riots took place during Reform agitation in Bristol in 1831. Such was the historical context in which *Barnaby Rudge* emerged.

This is a vast, panoramic novel through the complicated multi-stranded action of which the leading characters play out their destiny. The story involves the interconnections between various domestic groups, which explore the various mutually dependent levels of the social order. Sir John Chester, is an unpleasant Protestant aristocrat, probably based on Dickens' perceptions of Lord Chesterfield. He has a very strained relationship with his son, Edward, who loves Emma Haredale, the beautiful daughter of an eminent Catholic family. Slow witted John Willett, landlord of the Maypole, has a handsome, open-hearted son, Joe, who loves Dolly Varden, flirtatious daughter of Gabriel Varden the sturdy locksmith of London. Barnaby Rudge, the youthful simpleton, is the son of Rudge, steward to Reuben Haredale. There is much life in several of the minor characters. But what impresses the reader, and will stick in the mind long after the book is laid aside, are the tremendous scenes of the mob – a human tide which breaks its banks, sweeping away all before it.

Dickens sets the beginning of the action at the Maypole Inn, rural Essex in 1775. The regulars in the taproom talk over the tragic events which cast their shadow over the whole story – the murder of Reuben Haredale, a local Catholic squire, and his steward, Rudge. But things are not as they seem. The crime was committed by Rudge, and he constantly returns and extorts money from his wife. Dolly Varden rejects Joe Willett's advances and in despair he joins the army for service in America. Emma Haredale, niece of the murdered Reuben Haredale, is the daughter of Geoffrey Haredale, his brother. She loves Edward Chester, son of the vicious Sir Edward Chester. Their parents, unable to countenance religious differences, forbid the liaison, which continues in secret. Several years pass, as the widowed Mrs Rudge looks after her simple-minded teenage son, Barnaby, who is accompanied wherever he goes with his sinister black pet raven, Grip, who constantly croaks: "I'm a devil! I'm a devil!"

The personal religious theme is swept up into the public arena. Dickens gives epic treatment to the worst riots in British history, the 'No Popery' Gordon riots of summer 1780. The deranged Lord George Gordon MP, President of the Protestant Association, led a mob of some 60,000 through London, to present a petition to Parliament for the repeal of the Catholic Relief Act passed two years before to grant some modest civil rights to Catholics. The houses of Catholic families and their supporters were burned, chapels, prisons and public buildings (including the Bank of England) were attacked and 12,000 troops were required to restore order after ten days of turmoil in which seven hundred were killed and nearly five hundred arrested. A hundred and sixty were tried and twenty six executed. Gordon was tried for treason but acquitted. The characters in the novel are drawn into this human maelstrom.

Simon Tappertit, Varden's weasel-like apprentice, Hugh, ostler at the Maypole, Dennis the hangman and poor misguided Barnaby Rudge join the rioters. The splendid Maypole Inn is attacked and Haredale's house at Chigwell is burned. Old John Willett is stunned by these events, and he never really recovers. Emma Haredale and Dolly Varden are taken by the rioters, but they are rescued by Joe Willett, now home from seeing action in the Savannahs. Rudge's fearful crime is exposed and he is handed over to justice. Haredale kills Chester in a duel. Joe marries Dolly and Edward marries Emma. Mrs Rudge and Barnaby live in peaceful seclusion in the country.

But it is the mob scenes which continue to echo in the mind. And Dickens seems determined to show that it is the ignorance of the mob which allows them to be led on so dangerously. Throughout *Barnaby Rudge* the crowd is associated with darkness and ignorance. Much of it is significantly set at night. London is presented as a dark, gloomy, iron-hearted place – a labyrinth, breeding discontent. The world of the rioters is swarming with devils, real and metaphoric. Pervading all is the false religious cry the novelist discusses in the Preface, the cause few understood, and which the leaders perverted to their own distorted ambitions: "…the worst passions of the worst men were thus working in the dark, and the mantle of religion, assumed to cover the ugliest deformities, (and) threatening to become the shroud of all that was good and peaceful in society…" The ostensible cause of the rising is of little moment to some of the leaders. Gordon himself is a special case, but Gashford, his fawning secretary, and Tappertit represent the malcontented, lobbying anarchists which the novelist so loathed among contemporary political reformers. The attraction of this vague anarchy to the mass of the people, in Dickens' view, lies in the mysterious way it is presented:

> To surround anything, however monstrous or ridiculous, with an air of mystery, is to invest it with a secret charm, and power of attraction which to the crowd is irresistible. False priests, false prophets, false doctors, false patriots... veiling their proceedings in mystery, have always addressed themselves at an immense advantage to the popular credulity...

Later he indicates that it was the rumours attendant on the 'No Popery' cause which really attracted the masses: " ...vague rumours got abroad that in this Protestant Association a secret power was mustering against the government..." and again the element of conspiracy spreading like a nocturnal contagion is stressed: " ...all this was done... in the dark, and secret invitations to join the Great Protestant Association in defence of religion, life, and liberty, were dropped in the public ways... and pressed into the hands of those who trod the streets at night; when they glared from every wall, and shone on every post and pillar, so that stocks and stones appeared infected with the common fear, urging all men to join together blindfold in resistance of they knew not what... then mania spread indeed..." The association of blindness, darkness and mania are significant. The Lord Mayor himself comes to believe that "there are great people at the bottom of these riots." The mob is dangerous because its irresponsibility and grievances can be used by agitators. In this respect Gordon is a very dangerous man because though sincere about his cause, he is deluded. Yet, though deluded, he has an appeal to the people. The purport of Dickens' fable in *Barnaby Rudge* is that the greatest public enemy is indifference. Nobody cares about the people, nobody is interested in them, until the strange figure of Lord George Gordon appears on the scene.

The novelist makes quite explicit Gordon's awareness of his own hold on the people, and the idea of darkness, as a metaphor of the dark recesses of the mind and motive, is always present: "...The Protestants of Suffolk are goodly men and true. Though others of our countrymen have lost their way in the darkness, even as we, my lord, did lose our way on the road tonight, theirs is the light and glory," says Gashford to Lord George Gordon at the Maypole Inn, after a day's recruiting. Gordon seems unaware of what he does and says, but aware of his hold on the people. "Did I move them, Gashford?" he asks his secretary. "Move them, my lord! Move them. They cried to be led on against the papists... They roared like men possessed" Gashford answers. "But not by devils?" said his lord. "By devils! My Lord! by angels" comes the sycophantic answer. The devils are significant. Gashford goes on to tell Gordon what he said to the crowd, and to stress the power Gordon had over them. Gordon comments: "It's a great power. You're right. It is a great power... But – dear Gashford – did I really say all that?... It's a proud thing to lead the people, Gashford... They may cough, and jeer, and groan in Parliament, and call me fool and madman, but which of them can raise this human sea and make it swell and roar at pleasure?" The sea metaphor is significant, it calls up an image of the restless element, which agitators can raise seemingly at will. It occurs again in the mob scenes in *A Tale of Two Cities*.

Barnaby's simple goodness survives the taint of the dark city. We leave him, happy, free and a lasting help and comfort to his mother. He carries one of the main themes of the novel. He stands for love, loyalty and purity, and has obvious analogies with Dickens' other worthy simpletons and saviours – Newman Noggs, Mr Dick and Joe Gargery. The worldly, the 'knowing' seldom receive praise in Dickens' world. Strange mixture of originality and imitation that it is, *Barnaby Rudge* is important in Dickens' development – a study of human wickedness which does not shrink from admitting there are no easy solutions. The earlier Dickens had created characters – Samuel Pickwick, Mr Bownlowe, the Cheerybles – who seemed to be agents of a benign other-worldly power, who came on earth to put wrongs right. Varden is the nearest we get to this prototype here, he distributes gold to Joe and Dolly after the tragedies of the book are over. In *The Old Curiosity Shop* the gold-laden rescuer arrives too late to save Little Nell and Grandfather Trent. But now Dickens sees that men may be evil, the innocent may suffer, and the eyes of Heaven may look down, cold and indifferent.

7   Martin Chuzzlewit

The weakness in *Martin Chuzzlewit* is that the very strength of the novelist's invention seems to break out from under his control, to wander at will and refuse all attempts to contain it. It's an unsatisfactory novel as a work of art, but a book packed with writing wholly consistent with the true nature of its author's genius. The theme he proposed to handle was 'Selfishness' and "to show how selfishness propagates itself; and to what a grim giant it may grow from small beginnings." The balance and emphasis of the story changed as he began to develop it, characters took on lives of their own to the detriment of sound construction and for a mixture of reasons he packed the hero off to America.

Dickens uses the family context to lay out the leading themes of the narrative. We are early introduced to the memorable character, Seth Pecksniff, an architect at Salisbury, the epitome of hypocrisy. He has two daughters – Charity and Mercy. Cherry is a sour hard-faced creature, and Merry is a compulsive giggler. They live in hope they can entrap one of their father's pupils into marriage. He preaches the Christian virtues but unconvincingly. Pecksniff takes on pupils but makes no serious attempt to instruct them in their profession, but on the contrary, steals their ideas and sells their work as his own. One of them, John Westlock, has just been dismissed for disloyalty. Tom Pinch, who has been there for years, is loyally devoted to Pecksniff and blind to his faults.

When the novel opens, Pecksniff is expecting a new pupil – Martin Chuzzlewit, the grandson of rich old Martin Chuzzlewit, who is lying ill at the local hostelry, the Blue Dragon. His companion, the orphan Mary Graham, is in love with young Martin. Old Martin had hoped to match these two himself and feels thwarted that young Martin has himself taken the initiative. Tom Pinch sees Mary in the churchyard, and falls hopelessly in love with her himself.

Pecksniff takes Cherry and Merry to London. They stay at Todgers, a commercial boarding house near the Monument, in the City, which establishment – a mysterious world in its own right – is one of Dickens' immortal locations. It is run by Mrs Todgers, a kindly soul, who worries herself to death for the sake of her boarders and is obsessed with the quality of her gravy: "…a bony and hard-featured lady, with a row of curls in front of her head, shaped like little barrels of beer; and on top of it something made of net – you couldn't call it a cap exactly – which looked like a black cobweb." Here the Pecksniffs meet old Martin and his cousin, Anthony Chuzzlewit, who has a villainous son, Jonas, who flirts both with Cherry and Merry. The Pecksniff girls make a good impression on Todgers's young guests.

Old Martin desires Pecksniff to dismiss his grandson from his establishment, as a punishment for his precipitate wooing of his ward,

Mary Graham. As Pecksniff hopes to gain Chuzzlewit's money he is solicitous in obliging the old man. He is even conniving to marry Mary Graham himself to clinch matters.

Young Martin now resolves to seek his fortune in America and leaves, taking Mark Tapley, the ostler from the Blue Dragon, one of nature's optimists who wishes to put his good spirits to the test by enduring some of life's hard knocks. Old Martin seems to be falling under Pecksniff's influence, even to the extent of moving into his house in Salisbury. In the meantime Anthony Chuzzlewit dies in circumstances that might throw suspicion on Jonas Chuzzlewit. Cherry Pecksniff is furious when Jonas – despite flirting with her – then marries her sister, Merry.

An arch swindler, Montague Tigg, has in the meantime set up a vast fraudulent insurance business, the Anglo-Bengalee Disinterested Loan and Life Insurance Company, with impressive offices. He attempts to involve Jonas.

Meanwhile Martin and Mark find nothing but disappointment in America. He is fleeced in the deal for property, Eden, which turns out to be an uninhabitable swamp. He is taken ill but nursed back to health by the loyal Mark.

Montague Tigg believes there must be some secret associated with Jonas which would make him worth blackmailing. He discovers that Jonas had attempted to murder Anthony. In order to keep Tigg quiet, Jonas murders him and hides his body in a wood. This account of Jonas's state of mind – heightened to a state of electricity by the fearful crime he has committed – is utterly convincing and one of the most psychologically charged passages in Dickens' work.

Young Martin returns to England. He discovers Pecksniff about to lay the foundation stone of a building he, Martin, had designed. It is proved that Anthony Chuzzlewit died of a broken heart on realising how much Jonas conspired against him, but Jonas is arrested for the murder of Tigg. He commits suicide on the way to jail. Martin marries Mary Graham, John Westlock marries Tom Pinch's sister and Mark Tapley marries the widowed landlady of the Blue Dragon.

Dickens believed the strength of this work lay in its being so well constructed. Few readers would share his opinion. It is among the creakiest sentimental melodramas he ever evolved.

Seth Pecksniff as a picture of hypocrisy has few rivals. The portrait is touched in, time and again. The moment of Pecksniff's unmasking at the close of the novel, when old Martin knocks him to the ground with a blow of his stick, ascends to heights of ridiculous melodrama which surpass anything Dickens had yet written. He puts words in Pecksniff's mouth of sublime comicality:

> I have been struck this day... with a walking stick, which I have every reason to believe has knobs upon it: on that delicate and exquisite portion of the human anatomy, the brain. Several blows have been inflicted, Sir, without a walking-stick, upon that tenderer portion of my frame: my heart... And if you ever contemplate the silent tomb, Sir, which you will excuse me for entertaining some doubt of your doing, after the conduct which you have allowed yourself to be betrayed this day; if you ever contemplate the silent tomb, Sir, think of me. If you find yourself approaching to the silent tomb, Sir, think of me. If you should wish to have anything inscribed upon your silent tomb, Sir, let it be, that I – ah, my remorseful Sir! that I – the humble individual who has now the honour of reproaching you, forgave you. That I forgave you when my injuries were fresh, and when my bosom was newly wrung. It may be bitterness to you to hear it now, Sir, but you will live to seek a consolation in it...

Sarah Gamp, the hideous but compulsively and grotesquely amusing drunken old nurse and midwife is another of Dickens' memorable creations. She is called in to nurse Anthony Chuzzlewit, his loyal companion Chuffey and other characters, thus forming an important link to various parts of the plot, and serving to expose Jonas Chuzzlewit. But having brought her to life, Mrs Gamp then proceeds to have a life of her own, whose vigour and vitality exceed her modest role in the novel, but who nevertheless convinces us the minute we start to read of her. We never forget this fat old woman

> ...with a husky voice and a moist eye, which she had a remarkable power of turning up, and only showing the white of it. Having very little neck, it cost her some trouble to look over herself, if one may say so, at those to whom she talked. She wore a very rusty black gown, rather the worse for snuff... the face of Mrs Gamp – the nose in particular – was somewhat red and swollen, and it was difficult to enjoy her society without becoming conscious of a smell of spirits.

Dickens characterises the way she speaks so meticulously that once you have met her, you will actually always remember the sound of her voice:

> If it wasn't for the nerve a little sip of liquor gives me (I never was able to do more than taste it), I never could go through with what I sometimes has to do… leave the bottle over the chimley-piece, and don't ask me to take none, but let me put my lips to it when I am so dispoged…

Dickens is unstoppable – once his invention is engaged, there can be no restraint. Betsy has invented a fictitious colleague and confidante – Mrs Harris – whose authority she can colloquially invoke to boost Mrs Gamp's professional reputation. Of course, the nonexistence of Mrs Harris provides a superbly ridiculous moment of melodrama at the end of the novel.

There are numerous effective minor characters, such as the undertaker Mr Mould:

> We do good by stealth, and blush to have it mentioned in our little bills. How much consolation may I, even I… have diffused among my fellow creatures by means of my four long-tailed prancers, never harnessed under ten pund ten!

Augustus Moddle, the young boarder at Todger's who is hopelessly enamoured of Mercy Pecksniff, transfers his love to her sister, Cherry, jilts her and escapes to America. He blew his melancholy into a flute:

> He didn't blow much out of it, but that was all the better. If the two Miss Pecksniffs and Mrs Todgers had perished by spontaneous combustion, and the serenade had been in honour of their ashes, it would have been impossible to surpass the unutterable despair expressed in that one chorus, 'Go where glory waits thee.' It was a requiem, a dirge, a howl, a wail, a lament, an abstract of everything that is sorrowful and hideous in sound.

There is also Young Bailey, the boots at Todger's, whom we first meet as "a small boy with a large red head and no nose to speak of" the archetypal Dickensian Cockney lad, worldly wise beyond his years, who sustains the knocks and vicissitudes of life with commendable wit and fortitude, very much as we imagine Sam Weller must have been in youth. He rises in the world to become groom to the swindler Tigg Montague, is nearly killed in the fatal journey to Salisbury but who ends in triumph as partner to a barber – "what a life Young Bailey's was!"

The American scenes are in some ways difficult to accommodate. They are more satirically bitter than the *American Notes*, as by this time the novelist was aware of the hostile press this travel book had enjoyed in the Land of the Free, and he clearly lets his feeling have free reign. In their defence it could be argued that what he says about America is really no worse than what he says about his homeland, but thematically they seem out of place, although a strong case can be made to see them as part of the search-for-paradise-on-earth theme, which is quite strong in the novel.

The final verdict on *Martin Chuzzlewit* must be that without doubt it contains some of Dickens' most inspired writing, but that its parts are better than the sum of the whole.

8   *Dombey and Son*

The period of these early *Christmas Books* is a key to our understanding the major work which follows – *Dombey and Son*. These short fictions are the stepping stones which lead from the now clearly discernible 'early' Dickens of *Chuzzlewit* and the preceding works, and the obviously vastly more ambitious and mature work, *Dombey and Son*, and on to the major novels which follow. Dickens was already working on *A Christmas Carol* before *Chuzzlewit* was finished, and *The Haunted Man* coincided with the serialisation of *Dombey*. Dickens was here experimenting with style and form which was to lead him to that mastery of fable and symbol in the later novels, and this period in his life was one in which he returned deeply to his early years and mulled over the jarring experiences of his childhood. The theme of memory, time past and time yet to come, was in his mind from the beginning of the decade. In *The Old Curiosity Shop* there is a moment when Nell and Grandfather Trent pause to rest during their flight. It is evening:

> The child sat silently beneath a tree, hushed in her very breath by the stillness of the night… the time and place awoke reflection, and she thought with a quiet hope – less hope, perhaps, than resignation – on the past, the present and what was yet before her…

Dickens was experiencing what Steven Marcus has called "a massive return to the past." His letters are full of evidence of his constant dreams of the past. "My dreams are usually of twenty years ago", he wrote in a letter in 1851... "I often blend my present position with them, but very confusedly, whereas my life of twenty years ago is very distinctly represented..." His memory of childhood was very vivid. In the summer of 1838 a Dr Kunze had written to him for some details of his biography. The reply, dated July 1838, is a rather cocky and sprightly resume of his life and works, but it is extremely vivid on his childhood and days in journalism. When he came to write of Mrs Pipchin's establishment where young Paul Dombey is accommodated, he wrote to Forster: "I was there... I remember it well, and certainly understood it as well, as I do now..." In 1844 he wrote to his former schoolmaster, the Revd William Giles: "When I read your handwriting, I half believe I am a small boy again..." and in closing the letter he added: "I am half inclined to say now, 'If you please Sir, may I lave off' and if I could make a bow in writing, I should certainly do it..." His school-days were ever fresh in his mind. As Jung argued, we never free ourselves from our childhood, nor can we achieve this through intellectual knowledge. What is alone effective is a remembering that is also a re-experiencing. Our past leaves a great deal of material behind that is never really properly dealt with. We do not shake this off. We merely detach ourselves from it: "So that when, in later years, we return to the memories of childhood we find bits of our personalities still alive, which cling round us and suffuse us with the feeling of earlier times. Being still in their childhood state, these fragments are very powerful in their effect..." This would give considerable point to *A Christmas Carol*, a story in which the protagonist vows to live in the past, the present and the future. This may account for the intensity of Dickens' obvious personal involvement as he wrote it ("I wept and laughed, and wept again") and also for its impact on us, for he communicates a universal experience.

He was very conscious of the child figure at this time. Children feature powerfully in these Christmas novellas, and children are particularly associated with Christmas, not only because of presents, parties and other nursery ritual, but because symbolically of the vast hope invested in children in our culture. Many of these children in Dickens seem to have divine qualities. He was made "dark and cold" by the death of John Forster's brother in January 1844 and was reminded of the death of Mary Hogarth. It was during this time, in the mid 1840s, that Dickens told John Forster about his childhood and the awful blacking factory experiences. "Shall I leave you my life in manuscript when I die?" Dickens asked Forster in November 1846. He told Forster in August 1842 how deeply impressed he had been on reading one of his favourite poems, Tennyson's 'The Dream of Fair Women', which contains these lines:

> The smell of violets, hidden in the green,
> Pour'd back into my empty soul and frame
> The times when I remember to have been
> Joyful and free from blame...

In November 1843 he told Forster he had been greatly moved in reading Robert Browning's *A Blot on the 'Scutcheon*, especially with its thoughts on the "backward glance to youth" and the sections which idolise childhood innocence in the fond remembrances of brother and sister. These themes inform and animate *Dombey and Son*.

It was the novelist's original intention in this novel to examine the nature of pride, but in the event this work, as it developed, came to embrace far more. As the story opens, Paul Dombey, the rich London merchant, is anticipating that his life's ambitions are to be blessed with the arrival of a son who will continue the family line and the Dombey firm. He already has a daughter, Florence, who is about six when the story opens, but Dombey wants a son. He does not value his daughter very highly: "In the capital of the House's name and dignity, such a child was merely a piece of base coin that couldn't be invested – a bad boy – nothing more." Florence dearly loves her father and suffers his neglect. Mrs Dombey dies in childbirth and Dombey does his best to bring on his son, Paul, by all means that money can buy. He employs a wet nurse, Mrs Toodle, wife of a railway stoker, who lives amongst her numerous family in Staggs's Gardens (Camden Town). The name is significant. A Stag was a speculator who applies for an allocation of shares solely with a view to selling immediately at a profit. It was a vogue word in the 1840's as stagging was rife and frequently figures in cartoons and newspapers. Staggs's Gardens is destroyed when the railway connections for the Northern Line are built. Paul is not the kind of son Dombey wanted, not being strong, vigorous and ambitious at all, but thoughtful and dreamy and far too fond of his sister Florence for Dombey's liking.

We are introduced to the workings of Dombey's firm and the influence of his manager, Mr Carker, to whose judgement Dombey frequently defers. As the years pass, the cold and harsh atmosphere of Dombey's household is contrasted by that of Sol Gills', the ship's instrument maker, who runs a shop at the sign of the *Wooden Midshipman*. His colleagues are the eccentric old salt, Captain Cuttle, and Gills' nephew, Walter Gay, who is a clerk at Dombey's firm. Walter is keen on Florence. Dombey disapproves of any such liaison, and sends Walter out on the Firm's business to the West Indies. His ship, the *Son and Heir* founders and he is believed drowned. In the meantime, Paul is sent to boarding school but dies. Mr Dombey, determined to breed a son, marries the proud widow, Edith Granger. This alliance is negotiated to a considerable extent by Edith's mother, Mrs Skewton. It is obvious from the start that this is an arranged marriage with no genuine affection on either side.

Florence understands Mr Dombey's grief at the loss of young Paul and wants to show him even more affection. But her love is cruelly rejected. She makes good friends with Edith. As the breach in the Dombey marriage widens, Carker begins to be attracted to Edith. Unwittingly, Dombey asks Carker to act as go-between betwixt Dombey and his wife. In the meantime, Carker has been recklessly investing the firm's money in railway speculation. This is based on the financial panic of the mid 1840s brought on by over-speculation in railways. Staggs's Gardens is destroyed in the construction of the Northern Line into London (this parallels the actual construction of the Euston Line). Carker elopes with Edith, the firm goes bankrupt and Florence is driven from home by her father. She flees to the *Wooden Midshipman*, where Cuttle nurses her back to health. Walter returns safely, he had not been drowned after all. Walter and Florence are married. There is a convincing fairy-story element in the stories of these two characters – he is very much the Dick Whittington character, and she has more than a resemblance to Cinderella. The love of fairy and nursery tales was very strong in Dickens. John Forster records in his *Life of Charles Dickens*:

> No one was more intensely fond than Dickens of old nursery tales, and he had a secret delight in feeling that he was here only giving them a higher form. The social and manly virtues he desired to teach, were not less the charm of the ghost, the goblin, and the fairy fancies of his childhood... What now more to be conquered were the formidable dragons and giants that had their places at our own hearths...
>
> *Life of Charles Dickens*

Dombey now loses everything. Now completely reduced he haunts the empty mansion like a ghost. Here, Florence and her father are eventually reconciled. He is given a home with the couple and acts as a wonderful grandfather to their son.

Dickens was very proud of *Dombey and Son* and wrote to Forster in September 1849: "I have a strong belief, that if any of my books are read years hence, *Dombey* will be remembered as among the best of them..." Considerable evidence survives which gives us a good idea of Dickens' original intentions. There is a letter to Forster in July 1846 before the serialisation began, and the design for the monthly cover, for which some of the novelist's comments are extant, as well as his letters about the illustrations. He told Forster his first ideas for this novel were to show Dombey's anxiety that his son should be pushed on, but that Paul's natural affections would turn ever more towards his despised sister, Florence, even more so as he becomes mortally ill. After his death, when Florence tries to give her father all the love she thinks he needs, he will reject her even more firmly. The Toodle family were to hold the parts of the plot together. Walter Gay was originally intended to be a carefree lad whose character degenerates into dissipation, dishonesty and ruin. This was altered and Walter becomes a Dick Whittington character who makes good, and marries Florence. The cover which appeared consistently throughout as on the first number shows that the plan was constant in showing the rise and fall of the firm. This novel breaks away from his previous "life and adventures" model and is more of a social study. Thus is shadowed forth the theme of the novel, the line from fortune to catastrophe in the illustration. Dombey sits at the apex of the design, enthroned on a massive armchair, his dais a large cashbox, supported with a flowing structure of cashboxes, ledgers, court guides, directories, playing cards. On the right side the design is collapsing, representing the fall of the firm. This is the kind of dream-like memory chain we have seen before entwining Marley's Ghost in *A Christmas Carol*. These are the emblems of Dombey's world, speculative risk is represented in the playing-cards, an image of flimsiness and gambling, revealing the pun in the title "Dealings with the Firm of Dombey and Son." This we have seen before in Grandfather Trent. In the novel we see it again as Carker pores over his documents:

> The general action... pausing to look over a bundle of papers in his hand, dealing them round in various portions... dealing and sorting, and pondering by turns – would easily suggest some whimsical resemblance to a player at cards. The face of Mr

Carker... was in good keeping with such a fancy. It was the face of a man who studied his play, warily: who made himself master of all the strong and weak points of the game... who was crafty to find out what the other players held, and who never betrayed his own hand...

There at the bottom of the design is Dombey, strong and vigorous at the left side, weak and bowed at the right side, with the emblematic figures of Dick Whittington, clocks, watches and the sea which are to be recurring symbols of mortality, life, reconciliation and continuity in the novel. The image of the sea is presented to us at the outset of Dombey: "The earth was made for *Dombey and Son* to trade in, and the sun and moon were made to give them light. Rivers and seas were formed to float their ships..." At the moment of Mrs Dombey's death the image of the sea is recalled: "The doctor gently brushed the scattered ringlet of the child (Florence) aside from the face and mouth of the mother. Alas how calm they lay there; how little breath there was to stir them! Thus, clinging fast that slight spar within her arms, the mother drifted out upon the dark and unknown sea that rolls round all the world." The theme of mortality is presented in the opening contrast between father and son: "Dombey was about eight-and-forty years of age. Son about eight-and-forty minutes..." We note that Time and his brother Care have set some marks as on a tree that is to come down in good time, and that the baby Dombey's wrinkles are to be smoothed in preparation for Time's deeper operations. The theme of time is constantly represented in clocks and watches. Dombey jingles his watch chain waiting for the child to be born. Florence is conscious of her father's creaking boots and ticking watch. At the crisis at the bedside we can hear Dombey's and the doctor's watch ticking as if in a race. Dombey refers to his heavy gold watch during the christening. At Dr Blimber's Academy we can hear the grandfather clock ticking all the time. The sea is associated with Paul, who frequently thinks of the river and "how steadily it rolled away to the sea." He is obsessed with the image of the river which, he comes to believe, will never stop because it is to bear him away. He comes to know his medical attendants so well that he can tell them from the sounds of their watches. The idea of the sea begins to take possession of him as he weakens; "Now lay me down... How fast the river runs, between its green banks and rushes... But it's very near the sea. I hear the waves! They always said so!" Presently he says the motion of the boat upon the stream was lulling him to rest. At last it bears him away. The sea had always 'talked' to him. We are reminded of this at the close of the novel, when Florence and Walter are together at sea. She hears the sea and sits watching it from the deck. It makes her think of Paul:

> And the voices in the waves are always whispering to Florence, in their ceaseless murmuring, of love – of love, eternal and illimitable, not bounded by the confines of this world, or by the end of time, but ranging still, beyond the sea, beyond the sky, to the invisible country far away.

The sea, for Dickens, lay deep in the mind as a picture of that from which all life comes, and stands for the ceaseless ebb and flow of life. The idea of time and affairs of men is presented to us at the opening of the chapter which deals with the wreck of Dombey's business fortunes:

> ...the sea had ebbed and flowed, throughout a whole year, the winds and clouds had come and gone; the ceaseless work of Time had been performed, in storm and sunshine. Through a whole year, the tides of human chance and change had set in their allotted courses...

In the article 'The Long Voyage', published in *Household Words,* 31 December 1853, Dickens wrote:

> I stand upon a sea-shore, where the waves are years. They break and fall, and I may little heed them; but, with every wave the sea is rising, and I know that it will float me on this traveller's voyage at last...

In *Little Dorrit* he refers to: "the flowers, pale and unreal in the moonlight, (which) floated away upon the river; and thus do greater things that once were in our breasts, and near our hearts, flow from us to the eternal seas..." (Chapter 28). The sea holds the several strands of the novel together. It is obviously always in the background of Dombey's business. It is as essential here as it is to the analogous group at the *Wooden Midshipman's* shop. It is also used to point up the differences between the two enterprises. Dombey's business is presented to us as a vessel and the bankruptcy as a "wreck", Dombey is a stubborn captain who "would not listen to a word of warning that the ship he strained so hard against the storm was weak, and could not bear it" and when it founders, his staff flee like rats from a sinking ship. Against this is contrasted the sea-worthiness of the Wooden Midshipman which, Dickens tells us, partaking of the general nautical infection of Sol Gills' premises "seemed almost to become a snug, sea-going, ship-shape concern, wanting only good sea-room, in the event of an unexpected launch, to work its way securely, to any desert island in the world..." He had intended that the theme of the waves, the sea and its eternal message for us all, should continue right through to the end of *Dombey and Son*, but for reasons of space he had to omit the closing section, which showed the ageing white-haired Dombey and his grandchild at the shore:

> The white haired gentleman walks with the little boy, talks with him, helps him in his play... The voices in the waves speak low to him of Florence, day and night – plainest when he, his blooming daughter, and her husband, walk beside them in the evening, or sit at an open window, listening to their roar. They speak to him of Florence and his altered heart; of Florence and their ceaseless murmuring to her of the love, eternal and illimitable, extending still, beyond the sea, beyond the sky, to the invisible country far away. Never from the mighty sea may voices rise too late, to come between us and the unseen region on the other shore! Better, far better, that they whispered of that region in our childish ears, and the swift river hurried us away!

Dombey is full of such poetic touches. Look at the arrangements for Paul's wet-nurse. Dombey's son needs nourishing. Mother's milk is not forthcoming, therefore Dombey is simply obliged to purchase the sustenance nature provides the mammals. Here is the child, here is the breast: now let me pay you – but first let me tell you my terms. Feeding a child is negotiated as a business contract, as he examines her "marriage certificate, testimonials, and so forth." Among the conditions is the changing of her name in order further to formalise their relationship. Polly is far too lively a name: "While you are here, I must stipulate that you are known as – say as Richards – an ordinary name, and convenient..." And he insists that it is entirely to be a business of hire and wages, the intimacy is to cease immediately her services are no longer required. In Dombey's world a woman can bare her breast and feed a baby with her milk, take the money, and the relationship terminates.

The reduction of intimacies of human relationship reduced to the cash nexus is a leading theme of the novel. The analogy of the arranged marriage and prostitution is central here. Edith is prepared for the marriage market by her mother, Mrs Skewton. She has a cousin, Alice, who is seduced and then abandoned to a life of prostitution by her mother, Good Mrs Brown. The analogy is maintained by the fact it is Carker who runs away with Edith, and it had been Carker who ruined and discarded Alice. (Dickens was advised to cut down this aspect of his conception, but enough remains to piece it together). Dombey runs his family like a business. The *Wooden Midshipman's* business is run like a family. Polly Toodle knows instinctively and deeply from the beginning, something which Dombey does not learn until he has suffered and lost everything. She knows what love and sympathy are and she is touched straight away by Florence's need for affection:

> The child... was so gentle, so quiet, and uncomplaining... that Polly's heart was sore when she was left alone... her own motherly heart had been touched... and she felt, as the child did, that there was something of confidence and interest between them from that moment... And perhaps, unlearned as she was, she could have brought a dawning knowledge home to Mr Dombey... which would not then have struck him in the end like lightning...
>
> Chapter 3

Much of the undoubted power of *Dombey* results from the consistency of its imagining, of the relationship between its themes and their expression. Frederick Chapman, one of the publishing partners, said that Dickens told him when he intended to begin a book he would start by "getting hold of a central idea" which he then "revolved in his mind until he had thought the matter thoroughly out" and then he would make "a programme of his story with the characters" and finally "upon this skeleton story he set to work and gave it literary sinew, blood and life." *Dombey and Son* is the earliest of his novels which puts forth a coherent view of society and explores the dynamic of its interdependence and various working parts. Talking of Good Mother Brown and Alice and Mrs Skewton and Edith, Dickens asks: "were this miserable mother, and this miserable daughter only the reduction to their lowest grade, of certain social vices sometimes prevailing higher up? In this round world of circles within circles, do we make a weary journey from the high up grade to the low, to find at last that they lie close together, that the two extremes touch, and that our journey's end is but our starting place?" Edith notes that Mrs Brown was like "a distorted shadow of her mother."

9   *David Copperfield*

David Copperfield in considerable part, is autobiographical. While writing the opening number (it was serialised like other works) he told John Forster: "Though I know what I want to do, I am lumbering like a stage wagon." As he reached the version of the blacking factory episode – when David works washing and labelling wine-bottles – he commented "I really think I have done it ingeniously and with a very complicated interweaving of truth and fiction." Later episodes, such as the climax of the story of Ham and Steerforth, almost overwhelmed him. On 21 October 1850 he wrote to Forster: "I am within three pages of the shore, and am strangely divided, as usual in such cases, between sorrow and joy. Oh, my dear Forster, if I were to say half of what *Copperfield* makes me feel tonight, how strangely, even to you, I should be turned inside out! I seem to be sending some part of myself into the Shadowy World."

David Copperfield is so fresh, so brightly coloured and sparkling – for all its up and downs, its comicalities and villainies – that it is hard to credit it followed so hard upon the heels of dark and brooding *Dombey*. The previous novel had demonstrated a growing mastery of complex multi-stranded narrative, but *Copperfield* has a storyline of the utmost clarity and directness. The original title was: *The Personal History, Adventures, Experiences, and Observations of David Copperfield the Younger, of Blunderstone Rookery* (*which he never meant to be published on any account*). There are some interesting clues here. In the life-and-adventures-and-opinions there is a distinct echo of *Tristram Shandy*. He seems to be reverting to his 18th century models, but additionally there is the interesting reference to autobiographical elements which were to be kept secret – as of course they were at this time. The darker parts of the story were only known to Dickens himself, Forster and very few others. Nevertheless it must be acknowledged that this continues to be one of the most impressive of Dickens' novels. The vividness and vitality of the experience is translated into convincing and matchless prose, which seems to burn its way into the imagination of all readers.

The autobiographical tone is established by the opening words: "Whether I shall turn out to be the hero of my own life, or whether that station will be held by anybody else, these pages will show…" At the

Rookery, Blunderstone in Suffolk, a young widow, Mrs Copperfield, is expecting the birth of her child. She receives an unexpected visit from Betsy Trotwood, her late husband's aunt. Betsy anticipates confidently that the child will be a girl, as she disapproves of males. David's birth sends her off immediately.

David's early childhood with his mother and servant, Peggotty, is very happy. Mrs Copperfield is courted by Edward Murdstone, a rather sinister businessman. David spends a blissful holiday at Yarmouth with Peggotty's brother, Dan'l, who lives in a boat with an eccentric family – his pretty niece Emily, her cousin, Ham and the melancholy Mrs Gummidge ("I'm a lone, lorn creeture, and everythink goes contrairy with me... Yes, yes, I feel more than other people do, and I show it more. It's my misfortune").

When David returns, his mother and the dreaded Murdstone are married and his life darkens. Murdstone is a cruel stepfather, and his tyrannical sister, Jane, moves in and becomes housekeeper. Murdstone tries to beat his school lessons into him, and when young David fights back, he is dispatched to boarding school. The carrier, Barkis, who takes David there, curiously expresses his interest in marrying Peggotty by saying, "Tell her Barkis is willin" At school David is beaten by the sadistic Mr Creakle. He hero-worships the arrogant senior boy, James Steerforth. His mother bears Murdstone a child but then dies – the child does not outlive her. David is then removed from school and set to work washing and labelling bottles at Murdstone and Grinby's warehouse.

He is deeply humiliated by these experiences, but his life is enlivened by his association with Wilkins Micawber, with whose family he lodges. Micawber is a feckless optimist with a grandiloquence the comic equivalent of Samuel Johnson:

> Annual income twenty pounds, annual expenditure nineteen six, result happiness. Annual income twenty pounds, annual expenditure twenty pounds ought and six, result misery. The blossom is blighted, the leaf is withered, the God of day goes down upon the dreary scene, and – and in short you are forever floored. As I am!

The Micawbers leave London. David finds working for Murdstone intolerable. He runs away to Dover, to his eccentric aunt Betsy Trotwood, whom he has never met but is his only relative and only hope. Beneath her formidable exterior, Betsy is a compassionate soul, and she and her slightly barmy lodger, Mr Dick, take him in. David is begrimed from his journey, and his clothes tattered. He is bathed and dressed in some clothes of Mr Dick's, which are far too large for him. The Murdstones arrive to claim David. Murdstone is implacable in claiming his right to David. The confrontation between Murdstone and his sister, and Betsy and Mr Dick, over David's future is a typically Dickensian scene. Betsy appeals to Mr Dick, the simpleton: "What shall I do with this child?" and Mr Dick considers, hesitates, brightens and then says: "Have him measured for a suit of clothes directly." Betsy says that Mr Dick's common sense is "invaluable." Thus are the worldly and rational Murdstones routed by a harmless lunatic, an eccentric old lady and a child. (Mr Dick's warm good sense is much the same vintage as Joe Gargery's in the later novel, *Great Expectations.*).

Sunshine now enters David's life. He is sent to a pleasant school in Canterbury, with a kindly headmaster, Dr Strong. David lodges with the solicitor, Mr Wickfield, who has a charming daughter, Agnes. Wickfield is a pleasant man, with a weakness for drink. Wickfield's clerk is the creepy, slimy Uriah Heep, who tells David:

> Be 'umble, Uriah, says my father to me, and you'll get on. It was what was always being dinned into me at school; it's what goes down best. Be 'umble says my father, and you'll do! And really it ain't done bad.

David leaves school and has ambitions to become a lawyer. He meets up with Steerforth again and takes him to Yarmouth for the celebrations of Emily's engagement to Ham. Steerforth considers the Peggotty family distinctly beneath him. Agnes Wickfield has already warned David about Steerforth, but he pays no attention. Steerforth finds Emily very attractive, and persuades her to elope with him.

David serves his legal apprenticeship with Spenlow and Jorkins and falls in head over heels in love with Dora, Mr Spenlow's flighty young daughter. Daniel Peggotty is determined to search the four corners of the world for his Little Em'ly.

Micawber has become a clerk with Wickfield's firm. Uriah Heep has wormed his way into a partnership in Wickfield's business, keeping Wickfield in the dark and plying him with drink as he defrauds and ensnares more and more of the firm's clients. He even harbours designs of marrying Agnes Wickfield.

David and Dora marry. At first he is blissful, but Dora's butterfly charms scarcely compensate for a seriously immature personality and basic inefficiency in running a household. As a portrait of young married love these scenes are unequalled in their sensitive mixture of satiric comedy and genuine pathos. Martha Endell, who was a friend of Emily's at Yarmouth and who had been disgraced and gone to London as a prostitute, is able to help David and Daniel Peggotty to find Emily. She has been seduced and abandoned by Steerforth. Daniel intends to help her to a new start in Australia.

The villainies of Heep are exposed by David and Micawber. Dora dies in childbirth. There is a great storm at sea off Yarmouth in which Ham Peggotty is drowned while heroically trying to save the life of a passenger – James Steerforth. David leaves the country grief-stricken. When he returns, Aunt Betsy is instrumental in bringing Agnes Wickfield and David Copperfield together. The Micawbers emigrate to Australia. The novel ends with David's serenity in marriage to Agnes Wickfield.

But there is much more to *David Copperfield* than the novelist's displacing the anguish of personal paranoid experience. This is a deceptive novel. Beneath the blissful innocence of its finale, and the rooks cawing round the old cathedral at Canterbury, there is a deep, disturbing psychological quality which lingers in the imagination. The scenes of Murdstone's barbarities are haunting, and his insanely reasonable arithmetic problems have a startlingly surreal quality: "If I go into a cheese-monger's shop, and buy five thousand double-Gloucester cheeses at fourpence-halfpenny each, present payment... " Who would walk into a cheesemongers and buy five thousand cheeses? And the hysterically obsessive 'double Gloucester' specification is a peculiarly eccentric detail. But the actual cost of not producing the answer within a terrifyingly short space of time is the thrashing of a lifetime, out of all proportion to the offence. Equally dreamlike are the sunny innocent moments of retreat, the love and comfort of Peggotty, the stay in the boat at Yarmouth. But the hero has to grow up and face the world. He makes some catastrophic errors of judgement (Steerforth, Dora) and has to endure the pain of maturing, but after the storm he drifts serenely into harbour.

David Copperfield blends personal biography with social insight. With its deployment of the several threads of time, memory, chance and fortune, the past, the present and the future, this is a very revealing novel of middle-period Dickens. He described *David Copperfield* as "written memory." Here he is a successful and established writer, looking back into his past:

"I think the memory of most of us can go further back into such times than many of us suppose… " (Chapter 2). Later he writes: "I have been very fortunate in worldly matters; many men have worked much harder, and not succeeded half so well… Heaven knows I write this, in no spirit of self-laudation. The man who reviews his own life, as I do mine… had need to have been a good man indeed, if he would be spared the opportunities wasted…" (Chapter 42).

As in *Dombey*, he uses the sea as an emblem of time and memory. Writing of his mother's funeral, he says: "All this, I say, is yesterday's event. Events of later date have floated from me to the shore, where all forgotten things will reappear, but this stands like a high rock in the ocean." This is how he describes the passing of time during his courtship of Dora: "Weeks, months, seasons pass along. They seem little more than a summer day and a winter evening. Now, the Common where I walk with Dora is all in bloom, a field of bright gold; and now the unseen heather lies in mounds and bunches underneath a covering of snow. In a breath, the river that flows through our Sunday walks is sparkling in the summer sun, is ruffled by the winter wind, or thickened with drifting heaps of ice. Faster than ever river ran towards the sea, it flashes, darkens, and rolls away." (Chapter 43). Of the night Dora dies he says: "Ever rising from the sea of my remembrance, is the image of the dear child as I knew her first…"

Memory, in this novel, is not to be tamed. It is a wild and wilful agent which delights and disturbs as it waywardly decides: "As I rode back in the lonely night, the wind going by me like a restless memory…" he writes after seeing Agnes Wickfield, "I was not happy; but, thus far, I had faithfully set the seal upon the Past…" Like Scrooge, he does not recall the past, but sees it done, it happens again before him. He is in the scene with his former self. The structure of the novel, dealing as it does with past, the present and the future, as well as with a poignant subjunctive sense of what-might-have-been, is greatly strengthened by four strategically placed chapters – 'A Retrospect' (Chapter 18), 'Another Retrospect' (Chapter 43), 'Another Retrospect' (Chapter 53) and 'A Last Retrospect' (Chapter 64). Several times he says that his past "haunts" him, and refers to the characters in the story as "phantoms." David's sensation of viewing the ghosts of the past is exactly Scrooge's experience in *A Christmas Carol*: "Let me stand aside, to see the phantoms of those days go by me…" (Chapter 43). Thoughts and memories, occupants of the mind, themselves of the body and yet have a separate life of their own. At Blunderstone with Steerforth: " ...my occupation in my solitary pilgrimages was to recall every yard of the old road as I went along it, and to haunt the old spots... I haunted them, as my memory had often done, and lingered among them as my younger thoughts had lingered when I was far away..." (Chapter 22). Later in the novel he passes Mrs Steerforth's house, the mother of his admired school friend, now dead: "...my mind could not go by it and leave it, as my body did; and it usually awakened a long train of meditations... the ghosts of half-formed hopes, the broken shadows of disappointments..."

The sadness of this book is often remarked upon. This is particularly the result of that pervading sense of what might have been, that searing awareness of chance in life – the friend not met, the street not turned up, the decision not made – of that tormenting if-only, the subjunctive past. He looks in the flickering fire in the hearth, and thinks as the coals burn and break up:

> ...of the principal vicissitudes and separations that had marked my life. I had not seen a coal fire since I left England three years ago: though many a wood fire had I watched, as it crumbled into hoary ashes, and mingled with the feathery heap upon the earth, which not inaptly figured to me, in my despondency, my dead hopes. I could think of the past now, gravely, but not bitterly: and could contemplate the future in a brave spirit...
>
> Chapter 59

David Copperfield has two outstanding merits which have contributed to its lasting popularity. It is approachable and it deals with aspects of life which touch us all. While it is incontestably true that Dickens frequently seems to repeat various configurations of human experience, especially involving the cruel treatment of children, the loss of faith in the relationships between child and adult and the immediate resolution of complex domestic or social problems by individuals whom the world considers remote or daft, these patterns are repeated in *Copperfield* but with an authenticity readers seldom doubt.

10   *Bleak House*

Bleak House was Dickens' most elaborately plotted novel to date. Although clearly a vast satire on the law's delay, it combines several important themes which are constant in his work . These are presented metaphorically in the all-pervading images of fog, damp, mould and rain, and in the central terrifying image of contagious disease. Dickens presents modern society and its major institutions (politics, the law) as a vast, confused, stifling muddle, in which the various antagonistic layers of the severely separated social classes are interconnected in ways they do not suspect. The action moves from a stately home in the country, through law courts, lawyers' offices and provincial life, through to the darkest recesses of the slums. The mainspring of the plot is the endless suit in the Court of Chancery, to which parties from all layers of society, from the very highest to the most humble, are ineluctably drawn as to a vortex. Smallpox kills the pathetic crossing-sweeper, Jo, but it also infects Esther, who is the daughter of Lady Honoria Dedlock.

Dickens mixes narrative mode between first person and third person. The scene is set with the fog of the Chancery suit:

> London. Michaelmas Term lately over, and the Lord Chancellor sitting in Lincoln's Inn Hall. Implacable November weather. As much mud in the streets, as if the waters had but newly retired from the face of the earth... Smoke lowering down from the chimney-pots, making a soft black drizzle, with flakes of soot in it as big as full-grown snow-flakes – gone into mourning, one might imagine, for the death of the sun...
> Fog everywhere. Fog up the river, where it flows among the green aits and meadows; fog down the river, where it rolls defiled among the tiers of shipping, and the waterside pollution of a great and dirty city... at the very heart of the fog, sits the Lord High Chancellor in his Court of Chancery...
>
> Chapter 1

The case of Jarndyce and Jarndyce was concerned with a disputed will. It has been running for years. The benevolent John Jarndyce, through his solicitors, Kenge and Carboy, adopts two wards in Chancery – Ada Clare and Richard Carstone. Esther Summerson is Ada's companion. Jarndyce accommodates them at his home, Bleak House. This aspect of the narrative is told by Esther. Richard tries various professions – medicine, the army and the law – and is equally unsuccessful. But he is convinced that the lawsuit will be resolved and make him wealthy. In the meantime he falls in love with his cousin, Ada Clare. He becomes wholly absorbed in the complexities of the Jarndyce case.

They meet the mad Miss Flite, a fellow victim of Chancery, and spend the night in the household of the misguided philanthropist Mrs Jellyby, who spends more time and money in fruitless do-gooding in Africa than looking after her own family. They are introduced to Miss Flite's landlord, Krook, the rag-and-bone merchant, known as the 'Lord Chancellor'. The threads which connect up the various characters are spreading – Krook is also the landlord of Captain Hawdon, retired army officer, who is the friend of Jo, the crossing-sweeper, one of Dickens' most pathetic young characters:

> Name, Jo. Nothing else that he knows on. Don't know that everybody has two names. Never heerd of sich a think. Don't know that Jo is short for a larger name. Thinks it long enough for him. He don't find no fault with it. Spell it? No he can't spell it. No father, no mother, no friends. Never bin to school. What's home?…

Hawdon was the former lover of Lady Dedlock, but now, calling himself Nemo, he works as a legal document copyist. Esther Summerson, it is later to be revealed, is the illegitimate daughter of the liaison between Honoria Dedlock and Captain Hawdon.

William Guppy, a clerk at Kenge and Carboys, falls in love with Esther. While at Chesney Wold, the magnificent, gloomy and dank country mansion of Lord and Lady Dedlock, he notices a similarity between Esther and a portrait of Lady Honoria Dedlock. He proposes to Esther but is refused. He then begins to investigate Esther's origins.

Tulkinghorn, the Dedlock's lawyer, is amazed when in the process of business he shows the Dedlocks an affidavit. At the sight of the document Lady Dedlock faints. He begins to seek the cause and tracks down the copier of the document, whose name is merely Nemo. He finds the address at lodgings owned by Krook, but Nemo is dead of poison. No papers are discovered. Jo, who had received kindnesses from Nemo, gives evidence at Nemo's inquest. Tulkinghorn reports back to the Dedlocks. Lady Dedlock affects not to be interested. Tulkinghorn is now very suspicious. Esther has by now fallen in love with Allan Woodcourt, an army doctor. Tulkinghorn continues his investigations as he thinks he may find some cause to blackmail Lady Dedlock. He discovers that Jo received money from a veiled lady in black for showing her where Nemo was buried. Tulkinghorn uses George Rouncewell, son of the housekeeper at Chesney Wold, and Lady Dedlock's French maid, Hortense. Guessing who this mysterious lady must be, Tulkinghorn shows Jo a lady similarly dressed in black clothes like the mysterious woman who gave him money. He recognises the clothes but not the wearer – it is Lady Dedlock's maid in her mistress's clothes.

Guppy tells Lady Dedlock that he knows about Esther's parentage. Esther catches smallpox from her maid Charley, who caught it from Jo. Esther's face is now badly pitted by her illness. This causes her to give up hope of marrying Allan Woodcourt. Tulkinghorn had identified Jo as a likely source of information useful to him and hounded the pathetic youth, who was constantly told to "move on" by the authorities. Lady Dedlock meets Esther and acknowledges the relationship, but says they must never meet again for fear of the secret's being exposed. Tulkinghorn tightens his grip on Lady Dedlock and when he is found shot dead, George Rouncewell, who runs a shooting gallery, is suspected. Inspector Bucket, however, suspects Hortense, who had expected to be paid for the information she supplied about Lady Dedlock.

Jo eventually dies in one of those characteristic Dickensian moments which in the light of the academic classroom analysis to which they are so frequently subjected sounds extremely melodramatic, sentimental and ineffectual, but which – read in due course and in context – are quite moving. He is brought into George Rouncewell's shooting gallery by Allan Woodcourt, who tries to get him to recite the Lord's Prayer during his final moments. He dies after only managing a few words: "Dead! dead, your Majesty. Dead, my lords and gentlemen. Dead, Right Reverends and Wrong Reverends of every order. Dead, men and women, born with Heavenly compassion in your hearts. And dying thus around us every day."

Dickens' point, which he satirically makes with reference to Mrs Jellyby's extravagant interest in the welfare of far-flung parts of the globe, is that we should show compassion for our immediate neighbours and fellow human beings, instead of condemning them to life on the streets, in the slums or the workhouse. When he is brought in we are told that he was not an Indian or a savage from the jungle:

> ...he is not softened by distance and unfamiliarity; he is not a genuine foreign-grown savage; he is the ordinary home-grown article. Dirty, ugly, disagreeable... in body a common creature of the common streets, only in soul a heathen. Homely filth begrimes him, homely parasites devour him, homely sores are in

him, homely rags are on him: native ignorance, the growth of
English soil and climate, sinks his immortal nature lower than
the beasts that perish...

We should tend the needs of those nearer home, for we have rendered this
rich and fruitful country a veritable human jungle, and peopled it with a
starving, filthy and ignorant native population of our own countrymen.
(The same message was made by those social investigators who examined
the nature and causes of British urban poverty at the end of the 19th
century, such as William Booth, who in 1890 published his findings with
the satiric title *In Darkest England*.)

Lady Dedlock disappears from Chesney Wold and is found dead at
the grave of Captain Hawdon. The Jarndyce case drags to a close but the
entire estate is absorbed in the legal costs. Richard and Ada have been
secretly married, but Richard dies soon after hearing the news that his
hopes of a fortune are to come to nothing. Allan Woodcourt and Esther
are married.

Although when reduced to such a summary *Bleak House* seems a
mixture of melodrama and pantomime, (Esther's housekeeping earns her
the nickname 'Dame Durden' at Bleak House) its unremitting realism
rivals Dostoyevksy and its satiric spirit is exceeded only by Swift. Dickens'
mastery of his art is beyond dispute. He now displays the imagination of
a poet, from the power and confidence of the opening pages, through all
the utterly convincing location descriptions – Chesney Wold, always
associated with rain, damp and decaying aristocracy; the papers, rust,
rags, parchments, cobwebs and must at Krook's; the pestiferous and
obscene little courtyard burial ground where Hawdon is laid to rest; Tom-
all-Alone's, the black, dissipated street where Jo lives – this is a nation
suffering from some mortal illness which devours the body from within.
As you read some of the descriptions you fancy that you can actually
smell them. Vholes, Richard's gloomy legal adviser, has an office which
is squeezed up in a corner, and:

> ...blinks at a dead wall. Three feet of knotty floored dark passage
> bring the client to Mr Vhole's jet black door, in an angle
> profoundly dark on the brightest midsummer morning... Mr
> Vhole's chambers are on so small a scale, that one clerk can open
> the door without getting off his stool... A smell as of
> unwholesome sheep, blending with the smell of dust and must, is

referable to the nightly (and often daily) consumption of mutton fat in candles, and to the fretting of parchment forms and skins in greasy drawers. The atmosphere is otherwise stale and close...

Chapter 39

The satire is strongly aimed against the law, which Dickens had learned to fear and dislike since his days working there. He assures readers in the Preface to the original edition of *Bleak House* in 1853 that everything he recounted here about the Court of Chancery was true, and refers to a current Chancery suit which had been in progress over twenty years "in which twenty to thirty counsel have been known to appear at one time; in which costs have been incurred to the amount of seventy thousand pounds... which is no nearer to its termination now than when it was first begun... " Another long running case he refers to was commenced "before the close of the last century" – and it was still going on. Dickens almost certainly based the Jarndyce and Jarndyce case on the famous Jennens v. Jennens case, a dispute over the property of an intestate miser in Acton, Suffolk who died in 1798. As he writes in Chapter 39, the one great principle of English law is:

> ...to make business for itself. There is no other principle distinctly, certainly, and consistently maintained through all its narrow turnings. Viewed by this light it becomes a coherent scheme, and not the monstrous maze the laity are apt to think it. Let them but once clearly perceive that its grand principle is to make business for itself at their expense, and surely they will cease to grumble.

But *Bleak House* is much more than an attack on the law. In this novel Dickens combines into one coherent and convincing work of art, the dimensions – social and individual – which had informed *Dombey* and *Copperfield*. *Bleak House* shows how the various elements in the machinery of modern society are all interconnected and work together to stultify human fulfilment and happiness. In his vision Jo, who dies of fever, and Sir Leicester Dedlock are ultimately connected. It is no accident that the name Jarndyce calls up associations with that contagious infection, jaundice. Society is diseased, manifesting the symptoms of toxic infection. It was at this time that medical science was beginning to take seriously the spread of disease by infections. Disease is no respecter of class divisions. But the highest and the lowest are not only connected, they actually reflect each other. Krook's rag-and-bone shop, which recycles dirty old rubbish, reflects the Lord Chancellor's department, which functions in a similar fashion. As Krook says:

> You see I have so many things here... and all... wasting away and going to rack and ruin... I have so many old parchments and papers in my stock... And I have a liking for rust and must and cobwebs. And all's fish that comes into my net. And I can't bear to part with anything I once lay hold of... That's the way I've got the ill name of Chancery... I go and see my noble and learned brother every day, when he sits in the Inn... There's no great odds betwixt us. We both grub on in a muddle...

11 *Hard Times*

This curious novel was written mainly to increase the flagging sales of his weekly *Household Words*. It has one or two fine scenes, but compared to Dickens' major fictions, this is a feeble novel. Many critics, following F.R. Leavis' lavish but misguided praise, have proclaimed its virtues. It would be fairer to say that it demonstrates the limitations of Dickens' creativity than otherwise. Its brevity might indeed be a recommendation to some, but herein might lie a major source of its unsatisfactory qualities.

The initial presentation or description of character – especially Mr Gradgrind and Mr Bounderby – is excellent, but showing character in action is rather weak, like the inevitable working out of something quite mechanical. Dickens felt himself cramped writing it in brief, weekly instalments. Lack of space certainly restricted his imagination and gives a rather dry, unyielding performance which disadvantageously lacks the verve and electricity of Dickens at his best. It was planned as a savage attack on the materialists' and political economists' view of society. By way of preparation he visited Preston in January 1854 to witness the strike of cotton operatives (see 'On Strike' in *Household Words*, 11 February 1854) but was incapable convincingly of working this material into the texture of *Hard Times*. Despite his efforts to transform these Preston impressions into his fictional Coketown, he was unable to capture the tone of Northern life as vividly as he did metropolitan experience. The Coketown characters act and speak like stage northerners. He was not out of sympathy for the plight of the people. It was rather that he lacked the experience of living in Northern England. He used his life experiences to animate his characters and their situations: a visit to the 'North' was not adequate for this purpose.

The intention of *Hard Times* is to expose the danger of bringing children up with an emphasis on material and factual things at the expense of the fancy and imagination.

Thomas Gradgrind, a retired mill-owner of Coketown, brings up Louisa and Tom, his two children, and runs Coketown school according to his materialistic principles.

> Now what I want is, Facts. Teach these boys and girls nothing but Facts. Facts alone are wanted in life. Plant nothing else, and root out everything else. You can only form the minds of reasoning animals upon Facts: nothing else will ever be of any service to them...

This repressed upbringing turns Louisa and Tom into emotional cripples. Gradgrind is shocked at the lax manner in which Cissy Jupe, a clown's daughter, has been brought up, and – learning that her father has run away from the circus – he agrees to take the child in to his household.

Gradgrind's best friend is the self-proclaimed self-made man, Josiah Bounderby, who is forever bragging about having been abandoned by his mother and having to have made his own way to material success in a hard world. Louisa marries Bounderby, and Tom is given a job at Bounderby's bank. But Tom is soon in financial difficulties and steals money from the bank, putting the blame on the pathetic mill-hand, Stephen Blackpool, whose life is brought to despair by a drunken wife. Stephen has lost his job because he refuses to support the local strike. Tom tells him he may get employment at the bank and tells him to wait outside. This casts suspicion on Stephen when the robbery is discovered.

James Harthouse, a cynical aspiring politician visits Coketown and is attracted by Louisa and attempts to persuade her to run away with him. In one of the few really charged and successful scenes in the novel, Cissy Jupe warns Harthouse to leave Louisa alone. The divine child image of Cissy has already been well planted in the reader's imagination at the opening of the novel, as we see her surrounded by an aura of divine light, when Dickens associates her radiantly with pure sunlight. She appears at Harthouse's hotel room with the power and presence of an angel. Harthouse is rendered defenceless by this innocent child:

> ...Mr Harthouse ...if ever man found himself in the position of not knowing what to say, made the discovery beyond all question

that he was so circumstanced. The childlike ingenuousness with which his visitor spoke, her modest fearlessness, her truthfulness which put all artifice aside, her entire forgetfulness of herself in her earnest quiet holding to the object with which she had come… presented something in which he was so inexperienced, and against which he knew any of his usual weapons would fall powerless, that not a word could he rally to his relief.

In her distress, Louisa goes back to her father, who begins to realise the failure of his methods. Stephen Blackpool is fatally injured in an accident. Before he dies he says Tom Gradgrind can shed light on the crime. Tom dies abroad. Bounderby is exposed as a liar and hypocrite, when his mother is produced. We are given a glimpse of Gradgrind, reformed by suffering, "a white-haired decrepit man, making his facts and figures subservient to Faith, Hope, and Charity… "

Hard Times has a concentrated narrative. The result is certainly a clear storyline, but the themes are out of proportion to the mechanism of the plot, and there is a preachifying tone which makes *Hard Times* worthy but uncongenial. Because the imaginative afflatus is kept quite deliberately on a very short lead, Dickens' methods are made obvious, which is certainly not to this novel's advantage as a work of art.

12   *Little Dorrit*

This novel, serialised in monthly parts between December 1855 and June 1857, is one of the most complex and rewarding of Dickens' novels, whose stock among the canon has been consistently rising. It has an elaborate plot, with several interweaving narrative threads. Dickens combines several personal themes about which he felt strongly. The prison theme and the weak irresponsibility of parents are very strong, as is the theme of the child who assumes parental responsibilities. But these idiosyncratic obsessions are effectively combined with several leading public issues of the day, including several recent banking failures, the failure in the government's handling of the war with Russia and incompetence, corruption and nepotism in the civil service. These leading ideas are threaded on to an arresting narrative line which concerns the varying fortunes and experiences which beset the hero, Arthur Clennam, returning to his family after many years abroad, in the course of which he exposes family secrets and uncovers a longstanding injustice. *Little Dorrit* is slow moving and awkward, but if reading is persisted with the work is ultimately rewarding.

Little Dorrit opens in Marseilles. Here, in prison, Rigaud tells a fellow convict, Cavalletto, that he is to be tried for murdering his wife. Also in Marseilles is Arthur Clennam, returning from China after twenty years working at his father's tea business. His father has died and Arthur is coming home to London. At his mother's large, gloomy house he receives an equally gloomy welcome from his invalided and bible-obsessed mother. The house is empty, apart from the servant, Flintwich, (who seems to be in league with Mrs Clennam) and his wife, Affery. Arthur is taken with Amy Dorrit (Little Dorrit) who does sewing for Mrs Clennam. Her father, William Dorrit, was imprisoned in the Marshalsea for non-completion of a contract with a government Department, the Circumlocution Office, many years ago. In fact Amy was born in the Marshalsea, where her father shamelessly subsists on benevolence and gratuities from visitors and friends. He is known as the 'Father of the Marshalsea'. Amy gradually falls deeply in love with Arthur, but does not tell him about her father. Little Dorrit has a pretentious sister, Fanny, who dances on stage, a stupid brother, Tip and a loyal uncle, Frederick, who plays the clarinet in a theatre orchestra. Arthur begins to suspect that his family has somehow wronged Amy Dorrit, but Mrs Clennam forbids him to mention the topic again. Arthur attempts to help the Dorrits and makes fruitless enquiries about Dorrit's creditors at the Circumlocution Office:

> ...No public business of any kind could possibly be done at any time, without the acquiescence of the Circumlocution Office. Its finger was in the largest public pie, and in the smallest public tart. It was equally impossible to do the plainest right and undo the plainest wrong, without the express authority of the Circumlocution Office... Numbers of people were lost in the Circumlocution Office. Unfortunates with wrongs, or with projects for the general welfare... got referred at last to the Circumlocution Office, and never reappeared in the light of day. Boards sat upon them, secretaries minuted upon them, commissioners gabbled about them, clerks registered, entered, checked and ticked them off, and they melted away...

Arthur meets an inventor, Daniel Doyce, and goes into business with him. Through various associations, Arthur is introduced to the Merdle family. Mr Merdle is an immensely rich banker and financier with a scatty, snobbish wife. He decides to invest his capital with Merdle. Rigaud reappears in the story, secretly investigating the Clennam family, with a view to blackmail.

Fortunes are suddenly reversed. It is revealed that William Dorrit is heir to a vast fortune. He assumes all the social trappings and lives in conspicuous consumption. He leaves the Marshalsea a rich man. The Dorrits travel abroad in style. The Dorrit money is invested in Merdle's business ventures. At Mrs Merdle's dinner party William Dorrit suffers a mental relapse and thinks he is back at the Marshalsea, betraying his prison origins to all the shocked guests, as he welcomes them to the Marshalsea prison:

> Ladies and gentlemen, the duty – ha – devolves upon me of – hum – welcoming you to the Marshalsea. Welcome to the Marshalsea! The space is – ha – limited – limited – the parade might be wider; but you will find it apparently grow larger after a time – a time, ladies and gentlemen – and the air is, all things considered, very good. It blows over the – ha - Surrey hills… My child, ladies and gentlemen. My daughter. Born here!

He dies a few days later.

Arthur Clennam is ruined when Merdle's business catastrophically and scandalously collapses, and Merdle commits suicide (this was based on the notorious swindler John Sadleir, who committed suicide after the failure of his Tipperary Bank in 1856). Arthur is himself imprisoned in the Marshalsea. While he is lying there, ill, Amy visits him and nurses him back to health. He learns of her love for him but feels his poverty and her wealth now separate them. Rigaud confronts Mrs Clennam with his discoveries – Arthur is not her son, but the child of an illicit relationship between her husband and another woman. Mrs Clennam has brought the child up with strict severity in order to erase the sin punitively, and she has suppressed a codicil in her husband's will which had left thousands of pounds to the Dorrits. Their family fortunes have also disappeared in the Merdle scandal. Rigaud threatens he will tell Arthur unless she pays for his silence. Mrs Clennam is so shocked that she rises from her wheelchair and goes to the Marshalsea. She returns with Amy to plead with Rigaud but the Clennam household collapses. Rigaud is killed, a victim in the debris.

Amy Dorrit now has no fortune to offer him. He has nothing. They are free to marry. The wedding takes place in the church next to the Marshalsea prison, where Amy had been christened. They leave the church, and go quietly:

> ...down into the noisy streets, inseparable and blessed; and as they passed along in sunshine and in shade, the noisy and the eager, and the arrogant and the forward and the vain, fretted, and chafed, and made their usual uproar.

The construction of the complex plot, combines a high seriousness with satiric edge and rich comedy, especially in its minor characters. Concurrent with writing this novel was the less than fortunate reappearance of Maria Beadnell, (see Dickens and women – Chapter 1) who corporealises as Flora Finching, the old flame of Arthur Clennam, and returns to embarrass him.

Then there is the magnificent creation, Mr F's aunt, a relative of Flora's late husband. She is a deranged eccentric, given to grim taciturnity, interrupted by "a propensity to offer remarks in a deep warning voice, which, being totally uncalled for by anything said by anybody, and traceable to no association of ideas, confounded and terrified the mind." These interjections frequently have an admonishing quality, made more alarming by their unexpected utterance, such as: "There's milestones on the Dover road!" or "When we lived at Henley, Barnes's gander was stole by tinkers." The parallel between the hierarchy within the Marshalsea and the hierarchy in British society is subtly suggested and exploited, and as with *Bleak House* Dickens suggests that all layers of society, from the highest to lowest, are inextricably interconnected. As with *David Copperfield*, Dickens manages to recycle personal themes, fragments from his own childhood memories of neglect, humiliation, poverty, his ambiguous feelings about his father, and to commingle these strong emotional recollections with his anger at what he saw in contemporary society – snobbery, money-grubbing, the triumph of vested-interests, the failure of national government to run the country properly. At the same time, once it has gathered momentum, the story is gripping.

13   *Great Expectations*

Great Expectations was written for weekly serialisation. The idea came to him more or less complete, and he said he could see "the whole of a serial revolving on it, in a most singular and comic manner." It is revealing that he re-read *David Copperfield* at this stage to make sure he was not repeating himself, since *Great Expectations* is a deeply autobiographical novel, in effect, and rather more open as to its author's deeper personal psyche and its secrets.

The hero's early childhood sufferings and humiliations and his ruthless ambition to rise into the genteel classes are true to the facts of Dickens' early experiences. Pip's overwhelming love for Estella, and the feeling that this was not equally and generously returned are quite possibly (and in a way, sadly) true of his feelings for Ellen Ternan. It was a masterstroke to have Pip tell his own story, as Pip is more fully aware of himself as a person and in his relationships with others than previous Dickens' heroes. Also Dickens exploits narrative irony, as Pip in middle age – when we assume, looking back on his own life, he is telling the story to us – is a far less admirable character than he thinks he is. There is a mastery of narrative here which always reminds me, favourably, of Robert Browning's monologues.

Philip Pirrip, known simply as Pip, has been brought up by his shrewish sister and her simple but loving husband Joe Gargery, a blacksmith, on the Thames marshes. When Pip begins his story he has gone to the churchyard just before Christmas to visit his parents' graves. He is frightened by an escaped convict who asks him to bring him food and a file to free him of his leg irons. Pip gets a good hiding for being late when he gets home, but manages to steal food for the convict, including a meat pie.

When he sets out early the next morning, he is startled by another escaped convict, but takes the food and the file to his convict. At the Christmas dinner the next day Pip is terrified as the meal progresses that his crimes and raid on the pantry will be discovered before the company – Mr and Mrs Hubble, Uncle Pumplechook and Mr Wopsle, the pretentious parish clerk. He is saved at the very moment when the missing pie is called for by the fortuitous arrival of the soldiers looking for the escaped convicts. They call at the forge to have the handcuffs repaired by Joe.

At the moment of their recapture the two convicts fight, as there is obviously very bad blood between them. When the convicts are recaptured Pip's convict gallantly takes the blame for the theft so Pip is spared.

There is a very eccentric rich lady, Miss Havisham, living locally in a big house, where she has brought up an adopted daughter, Estella. She wants a young child to be taken there to play with Estella. Pip is taken there by Uncle Pumplechook, the wealthy, pompous, materialistic corn-chandler, who is a relative of Joe's. Pip finds that Miss Havisham lives in a house where time has stood still, surrounded by the decaying debris of her wedding day feast. She was jilted many years ago, and has not changed from her wedding gown, nor gone out of her house since that day. Mice gnaw at her wedding cake amid the decaying table clothes and cobweb-covered decorations. To entertain Miss Havisham Pip and Estella play cards. Estella humiliates Pip, calling him a coarse labouring boy, with coarse hands and a vulgar way of talking. Miss Havisham gets some curious pleasure from seeing Pip wounded in this way. He has a fight with a boy in her garden, the son of a relative of Miss Havisham's – whom he thrashes – and then goes home.

Although his pride is extremely hurt, Pip finds Estella irresistibly fascinating and attractive. At a later occasion at Miss Havisham's he sees her lawyer, Mr Jaggers, from London. Pip works in Joe's forge. Joe's journeyman is a ill-tempered young man named Orlick, who resents Pip. When he is older Pip is apprenticed to Joe as a blacksmith, his indentures are paid by Miss Havisham. Mrs Joe is savagely attacked by an unknown assailant and rendered an invalid. Pip is convinced that the deed was done by Orlick. Joe takes in the young orphan, Biddy, to be his housekeeper. Pip and Biddy become good friends and he confides in her his ambition to become a gentleman one day. He wants to be good enough to marry Estella, though he does not confess as much to Biddy.

Jaggers turns up at the forge and says he is acting under instructions from a client who does not wish to be named at this stage, but that Pip has 'great expectations' from a secret benefactor. Pip is to go to London and be trained to be a gentleman. He must always retain the name of Pip. He will be given an ample allowance and is never to seek to find out who his benefactor is. He buys new clothes, says farewell to Joe and Miss Havisham and leaves for London.

In London he lives in Barnard's Inn with Herbert Pocket, a nephew of Miss Havisham's, who is to be his mentor in London society. He recognises Herbert as the boy he had beaten in Miss Havisham's garden. Pip learns good manners, social decorum and mixes in good society. They get on very well together, and talk about Miss Havisham. Herbert tells him her story. The man who jilted her had got a great deal of money out of her, and her half-brother was partner to these transactions. Little is known about Estella. Pip is now convinced that he has read all the signs correctly, and that his expectations are from Miss Havisham, who is really grooming him for Estella:

> She had adopted Estella, she had as good as adopted me, and it
> could not fail to be her intention to bring us together. She reserved
> it to me to restore the desolate house, admit the sunshine into the
> dark rooms, set the clocks a going and the cold hearths a blazing…
> in short, do all the shining deeds of the Young Knight of romance,
> and marry the Princess.
>
> Chapter 29

Joe Gargery visits Pip and Herbert at their apartment in London. Pip is
ashamed and embarrassed by Joe's lack of sophistication and good
manners. Unwittingly, Pip has become an insufferable snob. Joe's brief
speech at parting is wonderfully inarticulate and confused but Joe directly
and sincerely speaks from his heart. To paraphrase the great Irish aphorist,
one would have to have a heart of stone not to be moved to hear Joe say:

> Pip, dear old chap, life is made up of ever so many partings welded
> together, as I may say, and one man's a blacksmith, and one's a
> whitesmith, and one's a goldsmith, and one's a coppersmith.
> Divisions among such must come, and must be met as they come.
> If there's been any fault at all today, it's mine. You and me is not
> two figures to be together in London; nor yet anywheres else but
> what is private, and beknown, and understood among friends. It
> ain't that I am proud, but that I want to be right, as you shall
> never see me no more in these clothes. I'm wrong in these clothes.
> I'm wrong out of the forge… You won't find half so much fault
> in me if you think of me in my forge dress, with my hammer in
> my hand, or even my pipe… I'm awful dull, but I hope I've beat
> out something nigh the right of this at last…
>
> Chapter 28

Pip is invited to dinner at Jaggers' place, where he meets a surly fellow,
Bentley Drummle, whom he dislikes. Jaggers' housekeeper is a woman
of about forty, with an impressive face. Miss Havisham calls him back to
the village where he meets Estella again. She is now home from finishing
her education in France. She is more beautiful than ever. Pip is perplexed
by a resemblance to a face he cannot actually place. Miss Havisham asks
him: "Is she beautiful, graceful, well-grown? Do you admire her?" She
puts her arm round Pip's neck and draws his head close to hers as she
vehemently says: "Love her, love her, love her! If she favours you, love

her. If she wounds you, love her. If she tears your heart to pieces – and as it gets older and stronger it will tear deeper – love her, love her, love her!"

Pip sees Estella frequently, but is always distanced by her. He reproaches her for encouraging the advances of Bentley Drummle. Pip's sister dies. He comes of age and his allowance is increased. One night, Pip's convict turns up. He is Abel Magwitch, on the run from transportation in Australia. He reveals himself as Pip's benefactor. He has made a fortune sheep-farming in Australia and vowed that he would put the money aside to make Pip a gentleman as repayment for Pip's kindness to him all those years ago.

Pip is shocked at the news. By returning to England, Magwitch has put his life at risk. Herbert and Pip will have to get him out of the country. Pip now learns the story of Miss Havisham. She had been cheated by her half-brother, Arthur Havisham, and Compeyson – who was the other convict on the marshes. Magwitch and Compeyson had worked as partners in some crimes involving passing forged bank notes, but when before the courts, Compeyson, who was well educated and spoke with a good accent, only got seven years, but rough and ready Magwitch got 14 years. Hence their animosity. Pip also pieces together Estella's story. She is the daughter of a murderess, who had been saved from the gallows by Jaggers. She is Jaggers' housekeeper. Miss Havisham wanted a child to adopt. Jaggers provided her with Estella. Magwitch is her father.

They plan to get Magwitch on a foreign steamer. Unbeknown to them, they are being watched by Orlick and Compeyson. Orlick has always hated Pip, whom he regarded as a rival in his love for Biddy. Pip is tricked into visiting an old lime-kiln on the marshes. Here Orlick intends to kill him. Pip is rescued by Herbert. The operation to get Magwitch out of the country is bungled. They are pursued by the authorities and in an accident with a steamer Compeyson is drowned and Magwitch severely injured. He dies in prison, but Pip is able to tell him that his daughter is safe.

Pip loses his fortune with Magwitch's death. His creditors press for payment. Pip now suffers from a collapse. Joe travels from Kent and nurses him through his delirium. Joe tells him that Miss Havisham has died. He now realises what a cruel snob he has been and that Joe was really his guardian angel. He resolves to make a clean breast of it all to Joe, and to confess how mistaken he had been in his ambitions. When he comes down to breakfast he finds Joe has already left. There is a note on the table:

Not wishful to intrude I have departured fur you are well again
dear Pip and will do better without Joe.
PS ever the best of friends.

Joe also leaves a receipt so that Pip will know his most immediately
pressing debts are paid.

Pip resolves to go to the forge and relieve himself of his feelings of
remorse and square things with Joe. He further intends to tell Biddy he
has learned his lesson, and to ask her to marry him. He returns to the old
forge on the marshes to find that Joe and Biddy have been married that
very day. Pip comes to an arrangement with his creditors and leaves the
country and joins Herbert in business in the East. Eleven years later he
returns to find Joe and Biddy have a son, whom they call Pip. He visits
Miss Havisham's house and meets Estella in the garden. He learns that
she married Bentley Drummle, who treated her very badly, but who has
been killed in riding accident. Pip and Estella are now united:

> I took her hand in mine, and we went out of the ruined place;
> and, as the morning mists had risen long ago when I first left the
> forge, so, the evening mists were rising now, and in all the broad
> expanse of tranquil light they showed to me, I saw no shadow of
> another parting from her.

This is the usual published ending, but is not how Dickens originally
intended the novel to end. He meant the novel to have an unresolved
cadence and had intended to write that Pip had heard about Estella's
marriage and misfortunes and that she had married a second time, a
Shropshire doctor. Pip was in London, walking in Piccadilly with young
Pip, when a servant comes up to him and asks if he would come and talk
to a lady in a carriage who wished to speak to him. It is Estella, who says:
"I am greatly changed, I know; but I thought you would like to shake
hands with Estella, too, Pip. Lift up that pretty child and let me kiss it!"
She obviously thinks the child is Pip's son. *Great Expectations* would
then have ended:

> I was very glad to have had the interview; for, in her face, and in
> her voice, and in her touch, she gave me the assurance, that
> suffering had been much stronger than Miss Havisham's teaching,
> and had given her a heart to understand what my heart used to
> be.

It was Dickens' friend, the popular fashionable novelist Edward Bulwer Lytton, who persuaded him that his readership would prefer a romantic happy ending. As he wrote to John Forster:

> You will be surprised to hear that I have changed the end of *Great Expectations* from after Pip's return to Joe's, and finding his little likeness there. Bulwer, who has been, as I think you know, extraordinarily taken by the book, so strongly urged it upon me, after reading the proofs, and supported his view with such good reasons that I resolved to make the change... I have put in as pretty a little piece of writing as I could, and I have no doubt the story will be more acceptable through the alteration.

Most serious readers of Dickens would agree that consequently this novel is flawed. The separation of Pip and Estella would seem the natural outcome of the book. But even though the need for the 'happy ending' triumphed, the impact of the work as it stands is considerable, and it must rate among his highest achievements.

This novel rehearses several major Dickensian themes. In the character relationships there are some very interesting parallels with his previous first-person autobiographical novel, *David Copperfield*. The characteristics may be transferred, but the relationship is very much the same. Pip's parents are Mr Murdstone and Clara Copperfield in reverse. Clara dies, Mrs Joe is attacked and received injuries from which she eventually dies. Both groups have a soft, protective parent. Clara's attempts to protect David from the wrathful sadism of Murdstone are brilliantly paralleled in Joe's efforts to come between Pip and Mrs Joe. In both crises a cane features very strongly. Both Murdstone and Mrs Joe have black hair and very dark eyes. Murdstone dominates Clara in much the same way that Mrs Joe dominates Joe. Miss Havisham in her relationship with Pip is a sinister version of Aunt Betsy's with David. Both ladies have been betrayed by their lovers. Both withdraw from the world. Betsy was petrified of fire. Miss Havisham dies as a result of fire. Pip, as David before him, is confronted with very difficult choices in terms of a sexual partner, this gives us the striking echo in the Dora and Agnes/Biddy and Estella group. Agnes and Biddy are idealised sister figures. Dora and Estella are erotic.

Pip, as narrator, in himself embodies the past, the present and the future. But he is placed in much sharper critical light than David. Dickens uses several figures in this novel in order to ridicule Pip by guying his behaviour.

Mr Wopsle, who expressed his ambitions to enter the church when we first meet him at the Gargery's Christmas meal, later enjoys ludicrous failure in an acting career. His desire to make something of himself in the world, shadows Pip's similar ambitions. The shop-boy at the town outfitters where Pip bought his posh clothes for London caricatures Pip. When Pip went back to the village he had tried to avoid seeing Joe Gargery. The boy mimics these snobbish airs, strutting along the pavement, with his shirt collar turned up á la mode, twirling imaginary side whiskers and ejaculating with a wave of his hand to the boys following him: "Don't know yah, don't know yah, 'pon my soul don't know yah!" Orlick is a dark parody of Pip. He is Pip's alter ego, in his form vengeance is committed upon the person of Mrs Joe. Orlick tells Pip when he holds him prisoner in the lime-kiln:

> I tell you it was your doing – I tell you it was done through you...
> I come upon her from behind... I giv' it her! I left her for dead...
> But it weren't Old Orlick as did it; it was you. You was favoured,
> and he was bullied and beat... You done it; now you pays for it.

The leading theme of *Great Expectations* is the destructive mechanism of the class system which not only thwarts human ambition, but wholly pulverises the human soul. Pip gradually learns, and as the novel closes we feel there is hope for him. But we have been shown a terrible portrait of modern society. Dickens presents this view of society in an impressive array of contrasting symbols – fire, warmth, animals, stars and jewellery. The warmth and glow of Joe's undying love is given us in the happy associations with firelight in the forge, and Joe's immense strength and gentleness. He lays his hand on Pip "with the touch of a woman" and Pip thinks of him, in his combination of strength and gentleness, like a steam-hammer, "that can crush a man or pat an egg-shell." The conversation at the Christmas dinner is all about animals, sparked off by the use of "pork" as a sermon text for Mr Wopsle. They speculate that if Pip had been born a pig he would have been slaughtered as a squealer by the local butcher. The convicts are described as "wild animals" and the hulks as "wicked Noah's arks." To Joe the convicts are "poor miserable fellow creatures." Jaggers warns Joe not to go from his words, having agreed to release Pip from his indentures, asking him if he keeps a dog: "Bear in mind then, that Brag is a good dog, but that Holdfast is a better." Stars are associated with coldness, distance and indifference. As Pip leaves Joe's to go to

Miss Havisham's the stars "twinkled out one by one, without throwing any light on the question why on earth I was going to play at Miss Havisham's..." Pip looks up at the stars on the way back from Miss Havisham's and "considered how awful it would be for a man to turn his face up to them as he froze to death, and see no help or pity in all the glittering multitude." The name Estella means 'star'. She has been brought up to be admired but not to respond with warm feeling. She is seen coming down the stairs with a candle in her hand looking "like a star" and Pip senses that she "looks down on him." When Pip tells the incredulous Joe and Mrs Joe the pack of lies about what had happened at Satis House, he says: "We played with flags... Estella waved a blue flag... and Miss Havisham waved one sprinkled all over with little gold stars..." Pip looks inconsolably up at the night sky from the forge door: "...for our kitchen door opened at once upon the night, and stood open on summer evenings to air the room. The very stars to which I then raised my eyes, I am afraid I took to be but poor and humble stars for glittering on the rustic objects among which I had passed my life." (Chapter 18). Later in the novel, when Pip is beginning to understand how adamantine Estella's heart has become, he walks about the gardens in Satis House "with a depressed heart ... in the starlight." Miss Havisham bedecks Estella "with some of the most beautiful jewels from her dressing table" which glitter and reflect the light as stars. As a socialite in London, Estella is seen wearing dazzling jewels. When Pip meets her in the final pages of the novel: "A cold silvery mist had veiled the afternoon, and the moon was not yet up to scatter it. But, the stars were shining beyond the mind, and the moon was coming, and the evening was not dark..." This is a society which admires precious stones, but treats human beings as less than animals.

14   *Our Mutual Friend*

This was Dickens' last completed novel again serialised in monthly parts. For several reasons, including the strain of his personal relation-ships with his wife and with Ellen Ternan, his reading tours, editorial duties and declining health, he found its composition rather hard going. In 1846 he had written: "Invention, thank God, seems the easiest thing in the world." Writing was accomplished very slowly, and during work on *Our Mutual Friend* he was always careful to be a few chapters ahead. But during the fourth number he wrote:

> Although I have not been wanting in industry, I have been wanting
> in invention, and have fallen back with the book. Looming large
> before me is the Christmas work, and I can hardly hope to do it
> without losing a number of *Our Mutual Friend*... This week I
> have been very unwell; am still out of sorts, and as I know from
> today's slow experience, have a very mountain to climb before I
> shall see the open country of my work.

Nevertheless, as far as the finished novel is concerned, the plotting
was as complex, the themes as elaborated, the characterisation as sharp,
the satire as pointed as ever. The comic zest and gusto of early Dickens
was gone, but that is not a sudden characteristic of *Our Mutual Friend*.
The vision had been darkening since the early 1850s, and symptoms were
already showing as early as *Dombey and Son*. In one respect there are
very strong links with his work in the 1840s, and that is in the theme of
muck and money. *Our Mutual Friend* is a monumental satire on a society
which worships money, which, Dickens suggests, in itself is worthless.
That useful phrase of Oscar Wilde's applies here. This is a society which
knows the price of everything, and the value of nothing. Money, in physical
terms is just round bits of metal and pieces of paper, but Dickens shows
how modern men and women spend their lives in its thrall. The great
metaphor which holds *Our Mutual Friend* together is the vast dust heap
which stands for a fortune.

These heaps of dust and rubbish were objects of great commercial
value. They were bought and sold because of the wealth they might yield
– from lost items of valuable property they might contain, and for the
marketable material which could be sifted from them – soot used as
manure, ashes used in brickmaking, bones and human excrement used in
fertiliser. In *Household Words* 13 July 1850 there is an article about the
sums of money which could be made out of dust heaps, sometimes as
much as between £40,000 or £50,000. Among the frightening sights the
last Spirit shows Scrooge is the den of a dealer in urban debris, situated
amid streets of filthy, stinking, dank, wretched houses in foul and narrow
streets, to which his miserable, grimy possessions are brought after his
death:

> ...a low-browed, beetling shop, below a pent-house roof, where
> iron, old rags, bottles, bones, and greasy offal, were bought. Upon
> the floor within, were piled up heaps of rusty keys, nails, chains,
> hinges, files, scales, weights, and refuse of all kinds. Secrets that

few would like to scrutinise were bred and hidden in mountains of unseemly rags, masses of corrupted fat, and sepulchres of bones.

Mr Merdle, the sordid money grubber of *Little Dorrit* has a name which is a pun on the French word for excrement. In *Hard Times* Dickens refers to Parliament as the "national dustmen" (*Hard Times*, Chapter 12). This string of images seems to expand the line in *Hamlet* where wealthy upstart Osric is characterised as "spacious in the possession of dirt." In *Our Mutual Friend* this theme is given a thorough work out. The theme of the book is money, money, money – and this triplet recurs throughout. Bella Wilfer tells her father that the whole life she places before herself is "money, money, money." Silas Wegg, convinced that Boffin has become possessed with the idea of money, hobbles about on his wooden leg, hammering out the rhythm with his wooden leg: "He's GROWN too FOND of MONEY for THAT, he's GROWN too FOND of MONEY." The cement which holds people together is money, money, money. Dust is money, and money is dust. In *Our Mutual Friend* the dust is everywhere, blown about on the wind, and people choke on it, just as human aspirations and wholesomeness becomes choked with materialism:

> It was not summer yet, but spring, and it was not gentle spring ethereally mild... but nipping spring with an easterly wind... The grating wind sawed rather than blew; and as it sawed, the sawdust whirled about the sawpit. Every street was a sawpit and there were no top-sawyers; every passenger was an under-sawyer, with the sawdust blinding him and choking him...

The wind, which blows scraps of paper here and there in London, creates an effect of it actually snowing money:

> That mysterious paper currency which circulates in London when the wind blows, gyrated here and there and everywhere. When can it come, whither can it go? It hangs on every bush, flutters in every tree... haunts every enclosure, drinks at every pump, cowers at every grating, shudders upon every plot of grass, seeks rest in vain behind the legions of iron rails...
>
> Chapter 12

The dust seems to invest the very texture of life in the city:

...such a black shrill city, combining the qualities of a smokey house and a scolding wife; such a gritty city; such a hopeless city; such a beleaguered city, invested by the great Marsh Forces of Essex and Kent...

Old John Harmon, the dust contractor, is dead when the novel opens, but it is his immense wealth, obtained from his vast accumulation of garbage, that sets the basic mechanism of the plot working:

He grew rich as a dust contractor, and lived in a hollow of a hilly country composed entirely of Dust. On his own small estate the growling old vagabond threw up his own mountain range, like an old volcano, and its geological formation was Dust. Coal-dust, vegetable-dust, bone-dust, crockery-dust, rough dust and sifted dust – all manner of Dust...

He leaves his vast fortune to his son, John Harmon, on condition he marry Bella Wilfer, the young minx-like daughter of Reginald ("The Cherub") Wilfer, the downtrodden clerk employed at Chicksey, Veneering and Stobbles. Bella was: "... a girl of about nineteen, with an exceedingly pretty figure and face, but with an impatient and petulant expression, both in her face and in her shoulders (which in her sex and age are very expressive of discontent)..."

John Harmon, son of Old Harmon, had been befriended when he was young by Nicodemus Boffin, his father's confidential clerk. If he does not fulfil the requirements of his father's will, and marry Bella, then the Harmon fortune will go to Boffin. John Harmon is uneasy about depriving Boffin of his inheritance. So he decides that when he returns from the Cape rather uncertain as to the destiny arranged for him under his father's will he will re-enter society incognito so as to assess the kind of future that might await him with Bella Wilfer. He agrees to change identity with the third mate of the ship, Julius Handford, whom he resembles. They change clothes and documents.

The mate then treacherously drugs and attacks Harmon and robs him. But Handford is in turn then attacked and robbed by others at the boarding-house. Both bodies are thrown into the Thames. Gaffer Hexham and Lizzie, his daughter, who earn a living by means of what they can fish out of the Thames, find the body of the mate, which from clothes and documents, is identified as being that of John Harmon.

We are now introduced to the Veneerings. Hamilton Veneering is the sole surviving partner of Chicksey, Veneering and Stobbles, the druggists. He has risen in the ranks of society, and is now insecurely lodged in the middle-classes, which fact is demonstrated in conspicuous consumption. He further establishes his social credentials by becoming an MP through the purchase of a rotten borough. He was: "...wavy-haired, dark, tending to corpulence, sly, mysterious, filmy – a kind of sufficiently well-looking veiled-prophet, not prophesying..."

The Veneerings represent New Money trying to pass as Old Money. (Veneering is the cabinet-maker's art of applying a surface of fine quality wood over coarser wood). Everything about the Veneerings is brand new. If they had a great-grandfather "he would have come home in matting from the Pantechnicon, without a scratch upon him, French polished to the crown of his head." The description of the Veneerings' banquet, which is where we first meet them, is in Dickens' finest satiric manner, and makes point after point with exquisite comicality.

The Veneerings snobbishly avail themselves of their acquaintance with Melvin Twemlow, a valuable commodity to them on account of his kinship with the aristocracy, through his cousin, Lord Snigsworth. Twemlow is: "Grey, dry, polite, susceptible to east wind. First-Gentleman-of-Europe collar and cravat, cheeks drawn in as if he had made a great effort to retire into himself some years ago, and had got so far and had never got any farther..." To them, Twemlow is an innocent piece of dinner furniture. When arranging a dinner party, they begin with him and add guests to him, so that he was like a table which could have a number of leaves pulled out of him: "Sometimes, the table consisted of Twemlow and half a dozen leaves; sometimes Twemlow and a dozen leaves; sometimes, Twemlow was pulled out to his utmost extent of twenty leaves." He was constantly perplexed by the fact that the numerous celebrities invited for show to dinner at the Veneerings, were claimed to be longstanding friends of the Veneerings, yet plainly did not know each other. He tried to puzzle this out but finally said to himself: "I must not think of this. This is enough to soften any man's brain...."

It is at such a party that Mortimer Lightwood, a young lawyer, narrates the tale of Old Harmon's wealth from the Dust Heap. He tells how how old Harmon had turned his son out of the house after he had protested at the treatment of his sister, for whom he had tried to arrange a marriage, and then threw her out when she protested she preferred another suitor. Young Harmon had gone to South Africa and made his own way in the world. When he died, old Harmon left a will with the conditions about inheritance depending on his marrying Bella Wilfer. At this moment he receives news that young John Harmon has been drowned. He goes to identify the body, accompanied by his friend, Eugene Wrayburn, a young barrister. On the way, they meet a young man named Julius Handford (who is, in fact, the young John Harmon).

Mr Boffin, who now manages the Harmon Estate, offers a reward of £10,000 for the apprehension of John Harmon's killer. Harmon keeps his identity hidden under the name John Rokesmith, and takes lodgings at the house of Bella's mother and father. He has the opportunity to see Bella at close quarters now and finds her very beautiful, but vain and spoilt. He gains employment as Boffin's secretary. Mrs Boffin is haunted by a likeness between Rokesmith and Old Harmon and the daughter. Bella Wilfer comes to live with Mr and Mrs Boffin.

John Rokesmith asks Bella to marry him, but she rejects him, saying she intends to marry money. Boffin, however, has recognised John as Harmon's son, and has come up with a plan to temper the steel in Bella's soul – he affects to become a miser and treats Rokesmith harshly for not looking after the affairs of the Estate properly. Boffin loses no opportunity to bring Bella's faults to her own eyes without her realising it. He says to her: "You have no call to be told to value yourself, my dear" and "You'll make money of your good looks." When Boffin learns of Rokesmith's hopes of marrying Bella, he says: "What are you, I should like to know?... This young lady was looking about the market for a good bid; she wasn't in to be snapped up by fellows who had no money to lay out; nothing to buy with." As Boffin points out, he who would hope to purchase a commodity such as Bella Wilfer must have the wherewithal: "What is due to this young lady is Money, and this young lady right well knows it... I know this young lady, and we all three know that it's Money she makes a stand for – money, money, money..."

This brings mercenary standards home to her, and causes her to reflect. In the end Boffin dismisses him. This touches Bella's heart, and she goes with him and they are married as Mr and Mrs John Rokesmith. Eventually the truth about John 'Rokesmith' comes out and with her help the schemes of Silas Wegg to blackmail Mr Boffin are exposed, and Boffin then inherits the Harmon Estate. In gratitude he keeps only 'Harmon Jail' (Old Harmon's house) and makes over all the money to John and Bella.

Dickens uses this main plot, and the parallel theme of the love rivalry between Eugene Wrayburn and Bradley Headstone for the heart of Lizzie Hexam, as a skeleton on which to hang the muscle and sinew of his satire on bourgeois society, including the story of the loveless marriage of Alfred Lammle and Sophronia Akershem. He had married her believing her to be rich. He is described as bright and shallow: "Too much nose in his face, too much ginger in his whiskers. Too much torso in his waistcoat, too much sparkle in his studs, his eyes, his buttons, his talk, and his teeth." Sophronia had married him believing him to be rich. She is a bird of prey, with "raven locks, and complexion that lights up when well-powdered – as it is – carrying on considerably in the captivation of young gentlemen." Then there is John Podsnap, a businessman very pleased with himself, who:

> stood very high in Mr Podsnap's opinion. Beginning with a good inheritance, he had married a good inheritance, and had thriven exceedingly in the Marine Insurance way, and was quite satisfied. He never could make out why everybody was not quite satisfied, and he felt conscious that he set a brilliant social example in being particularly well satisfied with most things, and, above all other things, with himself." Mrs Podsnap is like a rocking-horse: "hard features, majestic head-dress in which Podsnap has hung golden offerings." Then there is 'Fascination' Fledgeby the money-broker, who entangles people by buying up their bills. He was "the meanest cur existing, with a single pair of legs. And instinct... going largely on four legs, and reason always on two, meanness on four legs never attains the perfection of meanness on two.

Dickens is just as conscious of the effects of the class structure on human development, but he has moved on from ridiculing the aristocracy – there are no Verisophts, Mulbury Hawks, Dedlocks in his sights now – the focus in *Our Mutual Friend* is on the stultifying materialism and snobbery of the high bourgeois. Dickens' diagnosis of the condition of England slightly anticipates Matthew Arnold's celebrated professional opinion, *Culture and Anarchy*, based on articles he published in *Cornhill Magazine*, which appeared in book form in 1869. For Dickens, as for Arnold, the fear was that as aristocratic dominion of the nation declined and real power fell into the hands of the middle class it would be yielded by a class wholly unfit for leadership, ill prepared for civilised living. *Our Mutual Friend* shows a society whose sole aim is money and the pursuit of money, where people impoverish their souls in direct ratio as they increase their wealth and increase their possession. This is a world cluttered with useless things, where people are like objects because they are possessed by the things they own. The middle-class we are shown here, the ultimate model to which society aspires, lacks sweetness and light, is narrow, dull and puritanical. They are not so much wicked, as ignorant, shallow and narrow minded. A world with no ideals but plenty of cash, exemplified by the Promoter invited to dine at the Veneerings's, without "a sixpence eighteen months ago, who through the brilliancy of his genius in getting those shares issued at eighty-five, and buying them all up with no money and selling them at par for cash, has now three hundred and seventy-five thousand pounds."

This society is epitomised in the entitled 'Podsnappery' chapter, where the dinner conversation is ruined by the unfortunate introduction of the information that some half dozen people had lately died of starvation in the streets. Podsnap initially refuses to believe it and then adds that it must have been their own fault. The person who had unwittingly introduced this awkward topic to the discourse intimated:

> ...that truly it would seem from the facts as if starvation had been forced upon the culprits in question – as if, in their wretched manner, they had made their weak protests against it – as if they would rather not have been starved upon the whole, if perfectly agreeable to all parties.
>
> Book One, Chapter 11

The discussion then develops along lines which you will still hear in modern Britain. Today's Podsnaps can be heard declaring that there is no country in the world where better provision is made for the poor as in Britain today. (In 1996 government figures revealed that one in four children lives in poverty). At all costs centralisation must be resisted. Relief of the 'underprivileged' (as the poor are termed in today's political discourse) must be left to acts of charity. This is not the English way of doing things. Providence has declared that you shall have the poor always with you. Ultimately, it is not a suitable topic for after dinner conversation in select company.

15   Minor works

American Notes
Dickens and his family visited America in 1842. This had two important results – *American Notes* and the American scenes in *Martin Chuzzlewit*.

The same period spans the composition of the stories written for the Christmas market.

American Notes for General Circulation was based on Dickens' letters to friends such as Daniel Maclise, Thomas Beard and John Forster. The work was very popular in Britain but did not please readers the other side of the Atlantic. Not only was Dickens satirically observant of the sharp difference between the paradise promised by myth of the New World and the daily realities, but he was an outspoken Abolitionist – this more than 20 years before slavery was ended after the Civil War.

American Notes is still an entertaining read but is frankly, journalism. The zeal and comicality are as irresistible as the observation is idiosyncratic – pigs on Broadway, corruption in high places, the good humour of public officials, universal tobacco-chewing and expectoration. The apt turn of phrase never fails him – Washington is "the headquarters of tobacco tinctured saliva." Pittsburgh "is like Birmingham in England; at least its townspeople say so. Setting aside the streets, the shops, the houses, wagons, factories, public buildings, and population, perhaps it may be. It certainly has a great deal of smoke hanging about it, and is famous for its ironworks."

The book is riddled with extraordinary moments, such as Dickens' meeting, on the steamboat to St Louis, the chief of the Choctaw tribe. He spoke perfect English and was widely read, admiring in particular the poetry of Sir Walter Scott and James Fenimore Cooper's description of the 'Native Americans'. He was wearing ordinary everyday clothes, and Dickens expressed his regret at not seeing him dressed in his own attire, at which "he threw up his right arm, for a moment, as though he were brandishing some heavy weapon, and answered, as he let it fall again, that his race were losing many things beside their dress, and would soon be seen upon earth no more: but he wore it at home, he added proudly." The terrible institution of slavery is brought home at every turn, and reinforced by the reproduction of actual advertisements of missing slaves and slaves for sale. His feelings of unease at being waited on by slaves, human beings who are not paid for their employment, but owned by their employers, is chilling. *American Notes* is highly representative of Dickens' brilliance, exactitude and economy as a writer, and continues to come remarkably to life in the reader's mind.

Christmas Books

These novellas, written for the Christmas market – *A Christmas Carol* 1843, *The Chimes* 1844, *The Cricket on the Hearth* 1845, *The Battle of Life* 1846, and *The Haunted Man* and the *Ghost's Bargain* 1848 are usually found together in one volume, as *Christmas Books*. They combine pathos, social satire and comedy with homely, optimistic and uplifting thoughts suitable for the season which was at that time well underway into the massive media and commercial construction we now know as the 'Christmas Season'. The one undoubted masterpiece of this collection is the story of Scrooge, which miraculously combines the elements of both the traditional fairy-story and the modern novel.

A Christmas Carol, in a mere 70 pages, epitomises Dickens' fiction. It is the story of a selfish man, wickedly obsessed with money, who believes the purpose of life is to work and accumulate wealth, who is brought to realise his folly and suddenly repents. His heart is taken by storm. The composition of this story excited Dickens "in a most extraordinary manner" and he laughed and wept aloud as he wrote it. Scrooge is a tremendous creation.

He is a wonderful portrait of an overweening villainy, comically relishing its own wickedness: "If I could work my own will... every idiot who goes about with 'Merry Christmas' on his lips, should be boiled with his own pudding, and buried with a stake of holly through his heart!" When collectors call at his office to ask for charity to relieve the poor and destitute, he asks them if there are still prisons and workhouses and whether the Treadmill and the Poor Law are still in operation. He is assured that there these things are still in use: "Oh!" he answers: "I was afraid, from what you said at first, that something had occurred to stop them in their useful course..." The prose of this story is similarly packed with splendid gags – his clerk, Cratchit, at the office trying to warm his hands at the candle on his desk "in which effort, not being a man of strong imagination, he failed." Scrooge's apartments in a gloomy building up a yard "where it had so little business to be, that one could scarcely help fancying it must have run there when it was a young house, playing at hide-and-seek with other houses, and have forgotten the way out again." The plot is simplicity itself, but incorporates many of Dickens' themes. Scrooge is visited by several spirits who offer him one last chance to reform and to help to make the world a better place, by showing him his own past, the present, and the likely outcome of the future if current attitudes are maintained. His past reveals his solitary and unloved childhood and school days, his sacrifice of all things human in the ambition to get on and make money. The present shows him how ungenerous and unthinking an employer he is. The future shows the terrible consequences of his actions if persisted, shown him in terms of human suffering – the death of the Cratchit's child – and his own isolation – dramatically revealed to him by means of his own neglected grave. *A Christmas Carol* must not be underrated. It combines with a sure touch and masterful economy a considerable range of comedy, pathos, melodrama and in so many important ways characterises the true nature of his genius.

A Tale of Two Cities

The main theme of this French Revolutionary novel – the impact of long prison confinement on the sense of time – came to Dickens in the mid 1840s. He spent a long period of research and preparation in order to get the historical detail absolutely correct. In the event, this novel is strangely unsatisfying, and in some ways not really typical of the novelist's work. Nevertheless, when examined closely, several leading Dickensian themes are certainly visible, though his usual comic gusto is almost absent. Though alike in other respects, this marks its major difference from his only other historical novel, *Barnaby Rudge*. *A Tale of Two Cities* is a curious book, which is hard to credit as from the same man who had just completed *Little Dorrit*.

A Tale of Two Cities is crammed with most of Dickens' most renowned flaws – weak, unconvincing melodrama, mawkish sentimentality, theatrical dialogue, shallow characterisation, and shallow feeling. Apart from his obvious fear of mob violence, it has little to say in terms of social comment. The tedious nature of the plot is further rendered unattractive by the fact that it is very difficult to identify with any of the leading characters. The mainspring of the narrative is easily summarised: Charles, a good looking young French aristocrat, from a family held in particular loathing for sordid treatment of social inferiors before the Revolution, is arrested when he returns to France. His family have been attacked and their tax and rent collector, Gabelle, writes to England begging his help. He returns to France and is arrested and sentenced to death. His life is saved by Sydney Carton, a drunken and dissolute young lawyer, whom physically he resembles. Charles and Sydney both love Lucie Manette, daughter of a French doctor who had been imprisoned in the Bastille for many years before the Revolution. Sydney Carton smuggles Charles out of prison, and dies in his stead on the scaffold. He goes to his death with the words: "It is a far, far better thing that I do, than I have ever done; it is a far, far better rest that I go to than I have ever known." The one major impression left by this book is in the elemental sweep of the mob scenes. Despite the scenes inserted of the abuse of power by the aristocracy, to justify the rising of the French people, Dickens' Revolution is totally devoid of any shred of idealism. In correspondence he wrote of the "frightful oppression of the peasant" and "the condition of the peasant in France generally at that day was intolerable" but in *A Tale of Two Cities* we find little understanding of the common people. Sydney Carton martyrs himself to save the skin of an aristocrat, and the most memorable of the Revolutionaries is Madame Defarge: "A stout woman... with a watchful eye that seldom seemed to look at anything, a large hand heavily ringed, a steady face, strong features, and great composure of manner..." We take away a lasting memory of her, sitting at the front of the crowd at the guillotine, knitting steadily as the heads roll.

By the time we reach the sections where Defarge and his followers at the wine shop are plotting to rebel, and are adding names to the list of people to be revenged upon, it is all pure Tappertit and personal vendetta (Tappertit had 'pricked' the Maypole for destruction because it housed his rival, Joe Willet). The imagist effects of some parts of this novel are clumsy, and are possibly less effective for that reason, but they tell us a great deal about Dickens' imaginative conception of the revolution as something uncontrollable. When the revolution actually breaks, Dickens describes it in terms of a vast, wild, relentless and ferocious ocean. We may have been led to anticipate a storm, for the conversation at Defarge's wine-shop is of thunder, lightning, thunderbolts. Defarge is shown distributing weapons, giving orders, shouting execrations. The idea of the restless, mobile, liquid element is immediately established with the reference to lightning: "who gave them out, whence they last came... through what agency they crookedly quivered and jerked... over the heads of the crowd, like a kind of lightning, no eye in the throng could have told – but muskets were being distributed..." The preliminaries of the storm have passed and the irreversible tide is swelling. This is immediately followed by references to a "whirlpool of boiling waters" with Defarge as its "centre point" where "every human drop had a tendency to be sucked towards the vortex." The Revolution is presented in an extended metaphor of an elemental turbulence:

> With a roar that sounded as if all the breath in France had been shaped into the detested word (the Bastille), the living sea rose, wave upon wave, depth on depth, and overflowed the city to that point. Alarm-bells ringing, drums beating, the sea raging and thundering on its new beach, the attack began.
>
> Chapter 21

These images of surging, tossing, raging waters continue throughout this sequence. Prisoners of the Bastille are "released by the storm." Defarge, ostensibly the captain of this venture, is tossed ashore by the raging crowds at the Bastille: "so resistless was the force of the ocean bearing him on, that even to draw his breath or turn his head was as impracticable as if he had been struggling in the surf at the South Sea until he was landed in the outer courtyard of the Bastille..."

Indeed it is only in these crowd scenes that *A Tale of Two Cities* really comes to life. Interest in this curious novel has mainly been maintained by film and media treatment which finds the melodrama the very stuff of straightforward popular entertainment.

The Mystery of Edwin Drood

This was to have been Dickens' fifteenth novel, which was unfinished when he died in June 1870. He began it at Gad's Hill in October 1869, and wrote the last words of it on 8 June 1870. Its serialisation began on 1 April 1870 and the sixth monthly part appeared in September 1870. From these six episodes it is not possible – though many have tried – to piece together a satisfactory completion. We have some idea of the themes in Dickens' mind. He told John Forster that the leading idea was to be:

> Two people – boy or girl, or very young, going apart from one another, pledged to be married after many years – at the end of the book. The interest to arise out of the tracing of their separate ways, and the impossibility of telling what will be done with that impending fate.

This original theme was seriously altered when another idea occurred to him: "A very curious new idea" as he described it about the murder of a young man by his uncle. The murder would look back on his past crime as he sat in the condemned cell, and it would seem as if it had been committed by someone else. Soon after committing the crime, he would learn that it was unnecessary. The crime was to be discovered by means of a gold ring which survived quicklime. We do not know to what extent he changed from his original ideas. We only have half the novel, which renders speculation on the existing fragment completely fruitless.

Edwin Drood is unlike anything he had previously written. He is trying to write a mystery in the manner of Wilkie Collins, and there are things in *Drood* which remind one of the earlier *Christmas Books*, but the writing is extremely fresh and lively – wholly unlike the ponderous, satiric manner of *Our Mutual Friend*. The action is based in the city of Rochester, which he calls Cloisterham:

> ...A city of another and a bygone time is Cloisterham, with its hoarse Cathedral bell, its hoarse rooks hovering about the Cathedral tower... Fragments of old wall, saint's chapel, chapter-house, convent and monastery, have got incongruously or obstructively built into many of its houses and gardens... All things in it are of the past...

The novel begins with a curious Prologue, written in the manner of a drugged dream. John Jasper, choirmaster at Cloisterham, is dreaming in an opium den. He sees an Eastern procession and as he wakes the bedposts seem like the Cathedral towers. The Eastern element was doubtless to have a central significance in *Edwin Drood*, which Dickens was unable fully to elaborate before he died. Jasper's addiction is not his only secret. He has a concealed passion for Rosa Bud, who is betrothed to his nephew, Edwin Drood. Both Edwin and Rosa are orphans. Jasper is Edwin's guardian. Rosa is at school in Cloisterham, and her guardian is Grewgious, a lawyer in London. Edwin, an engineering student, comes to Cloisterham to visit.

There is a strange incident at a musical party, where Rosa sings to Jasper's piano accompaniment. Rosa feels herself to be hypnotised by Jasper. When he strikes a chord on the piano, she feels that he himself is in the sounds. She says he is: "...whispering that he pursues me as a lover, and commanding me to keep his secret. I avoid his eyes, but he forces me to see them without looking at them. Even when his gaze comes over me... and he seems to wander away unto a frightful sort of dream in which he threatens me most, he obliges me to know it, and to know that he is sitting close at my side, more terrible to me than ever..."

Edwin and Rosa realise that their union is not bound by real love, and decide to be as good friends, brother and sister. This is not understood at this time by John Jasper. Helena and Neville Landless, twins from Ceylon, arrive in Cloisterham. Neville is to be a pupil of a local clergyman, and Helena, is to attend school, where she becomes friendly with Rosa. Neville becomes attracted to Rosa, and she begins to resist the hold that Edwin seems to have over her.

The two young men quarrel, and while pretending to smooth things over, John Jasper actually increases their mutual animosity. But they agree to a meeting of reconciliation at John Jasper's rooms on Christmas Eve. Edwin Drood then disappears. His watch and tiepin are found, in a strange way by the clergyman who teaches Neville. He seems to have been drawn to the site by a kind of magnetism. But Drood's body is never recovered. Jasper was seen, the night Drood disappears, wearing a long black scarf.

Neville is arrested on suspicion of murder, but released for lack of evidence. When Jasper is told that Edwin's engagement to Rosa had been broken off before Edwin had disappeared, Jasper is overcome. Months pass. Neville is compelled to leave Cloisterham for London because he is hounded with suspicion and rumour. Jasper then makes an extraordinary declaration of love to Rosa Bud, swearing that he will hound Neville Landless to his death, unless she yield to him. She flees to Grewgious in London, and the fragment ends with the appearance of a new character at Cloisterham, Dick Datchery: "A white haired personage, with black eyebrows. Being buttoned up in a tightish blue surtout, with a buff waistcoat and grey trousers, he had something of a military air..."

There is something strange about Datchery. Is he someone else in disguise? Was Drood really not killed, and is Datchery really Drood, returned to spy on his would-be killer? We shall never know. Dickens took the mystery of Edwin Drood with him to the grave.

CRITICAL OVERVIEW

...His fun is a form of poetry; and quite as personal and indefinable as poetry. Like poetry, it is for the moment on one note, and making the most of one notion: like poetry, it leaves us amazed at what can be made out of one notion. That is what critics mean when they say it is not like life; because it is more living than life. It is a magic accelerating growth; so that one seed out of a thousand seeds of fact visibly springs and sprouts into a tree, as in a fairy-tale. Certainly this is not dealing with all the facts; but it is releasing all the potential life in one of them. Dickens saw something, whether in a man's notions or his nose, which could be developed more than dull life dares to develop it. The Dickens comic character is in that sense real and in that sense unreal. We may call it a caricature; though indeed it is a caricature of Dickens to call him a caricaturist...

> G. K. Chesterton: 'Charles Dickens', *The Great Victorians*, edited by H. J. Massingham and Hugh Massingham 1932

Charles Dickens, in his 'Boz' days, was able successfully to launch himself on the swelling tide of popular printing, publishing and the increase in popular literacy. Ordinary people were taught to read in very large numbers by the Sunday School movement long before national legislators manifested sufficient interest to pass the Education Act in 1870. During the same period there were developments in the technology of literary production and an increasing market as a result of rapid developments in transport.

Additionally Dickens possessed from the earliest days of his authorship an ability to perceive and exploit current trends in taste and fashion. This meant right from the start, Dickens was more than just a literary phenomenon. His stories were adapted for the stage as soon as they appeared in print. He was a public figure, associated with social and political reform – poor relief, education, saving 'fallen women', supporting ragged schools, literary charities, the treatment of mentally ill people etc – in his fiction and personally by taking part in reforming efforts and by constantly speaking on public platforms. He acted on stage both privately and for the public. He was a journalist and a public performer of his own works. His image, characters from his novels, jokes and puns about his name, personality and fiction became, from the very first, absorbed into popular discourse in advertising copy and iconography. "Blow me if that ain't Charles Dickens!" shouted a young boy recognising him in the crowd in rural Wales. Change the name to other popular writers – Bulwer Lytton, J.P.R. James, Harrison Ainsworth – and the point is immediately made: Dickens completely entered the bloodstream of the national culture at a very early stage, long before newspaper photographs turned people into celebrities. His death eclipsed the "harmless gaiety of nations."

Several qualities combine which it is easy to take for granted. There was much of the journalist in Dickens' art. Like a journalist he always endeavoured to give readers the kind of copy they wanted. But of course, it is rather more complex. He was a creative and original writer, who contributed to the art of the novel and to literature generally, but he was unusual in this important respect. He was deeply conscious of his work, of its shape, sound and sense – as are all true writers. But there are various ways in which writers are aware – and Dickens' awareness is of particular interest. It plays a large part in the nature of his art. He was a natural born actor. We know from the evidence of his family, that he frequently practised the dialogue of his characters aloud while looking at himself in a mirror as he grimaced and altered his face to meaning in the manner of a stage performer. He read his works to friends. (There is a detailed account of his reading *The Chimes* to a group of friends.) He created his works as public readings. He wanted to reach and to move his audiences personally. And to this end, he was – like a journalist – anxious as far as possible within the bounds of his creative intentions, to give his public what they wanted. He actually responded to his public during the serialisation of his novels. From his earliest excursions into lengthy plots we can see that he planned his fiction to fit in with the seasons. Dickens composed the unfolding narrative of *Pickwick Papers* with a deliberate awareness of his readers' sense of the passing of the seasons. In much the same way as radio and television today calendarise our experience, he imagines the action as the period between March 1822 and October 1828. The main sequences would reinforce the shape of the year. The writer seems to think himself into his readers' recent experience of time passed. As they read the monthly episode and recreate in their imaginations the scenes he has invented, they will naturally draw on their own experience. Thus we have the cricket match played in June, the shooting sequence in October. The Pickwickians go skating on the ice in February. Readers would enjoy the idyll of Christmas at Dingley Dell in the January issue, and the glorious colours of August in the September number. In the March issue, Sam

Weller sent his Valentine. It's on a fine October day that Samuel Pickwick sets forth at Grays Inn – in the November issue. He scooped the market with his *Christmas Stories – A Christmas Carol* was a publishing sensation of its time. The Christmas edition of a serial invariably provided happy and cheerful events suitable for the season – in *Dombey and Son* he saves Walter Gay from shipwreck in order to marry Florence, the young heroine. Cautioned by his publishers as to the acceptability of developing the parallel between the marriage of convenience of Edith and Mr Dombey and the life of prostitution to which her cousin Alice is reduced, he altered the course of *Dombey and Son.* He serialised *Hard Times* in 'All the Year Roun' to help its flagging sales. I believe this awareness of his audience was with him throughout his career to the end, and shaped, textured and conditioned the nature of his art. We should note that he confessed as much in the moving and sincere speech he gave at his very last public reading only three months before he died. He concluded by saying that he had had the honour of presenting his own cherished ideas before his audiences for their recognition; and, in closely observing their reception of them, "had enjoyed an amount of artistic delight and instruction" which he thought had been given to few men to know. Like all great communicators, he was almost instinctively aware that communication is in essence a two-way process. He watched his audiences, listened to them, and responded to them. That is why his novels go on speaking to us and why we continue to be ready to listen to them.

1   Dickens in modern times

This supra-literary immortality continued into the twentieth century. Bransby Williams's music-hall characterizations, Edwardian stage productions, Christmas cards, films, radio serials, cigarette cards, Emlyn Williams' readings, musical shows, stage adaptations at the Royal Shakespeare Company, BBC TV classic serializations, endless paper-back editions of his works, his face on our very national currency – Charles Dickens cannot be assessed simply and solely as a novelist. He is undeniably much more. His reputation was always furthered by his vitality in other aspects of national and popular culture. Although he has achieved mythological stature in the national consciousness, and his characters continue to be universally recognisable, it needs to be insisted – despite the frequent glib claims – his genius is essentially literary. Many continue to circulate the assertions of the early film-makers D.W. Griffith and

Sergei Eisenstein to the effect that his art was basically cinematic. It is considered enough to refer to the passage in *A Christmas Carol* where the last ghost's robe changes back:

> Holding up his hands in one last prayer to have his fate reversed, he saw an alteration in the Phantom's hood and dress. It shrank, collapsed, and dwindled down into a bedpost... Yes! and the bedpost was his own! The bed was his own, the room was his own...

This, it is argued, demonstrates that Dickens was a putative film maker, and this the prototype of a film 'dissolve'. It is revealing to explore our attempts to accommodate Dickens to modern modes of production and consumption. Dickens' stock in trade was words. Dickens was the first English novelist consistently to use symbols and images. This gives his novels not only a peculiar poetic power which haunts the imagination, and contributes to the unique quality of Dickens' authorship, but it gives the novels a certain individual quality: although *Bleak House* and *Great Expectations* are unmistakably Dickensian, they are also unmistakably different novels.

The atmosphere of *Bleak House* is tenebrous, musty, languid, oppressive. *Great Expectations* is quite different. This novel is held together with groups of contrasting images – the warmth and comfort of the fire associated with Joe and the forge, with the inhuman whiteness and cold, glistening stellar qualities of Miss Havisham and Estella. Convicts and children are treated like animals. This is a society indifferent to human warmth and affection, where life is cheap and jewels are priceless... Dickens is a poet. His mind seems to work metaphorically. It may have come from his reading of Shakespeare. It may have been his response to the challenge and opportunities of serial publication. Symbolism and imagery might serve to give coherence and consistency to a narrative extended over eighteen months. Imaginatively suggestive imagery and symbolism of this powerful literary kind is very difficult to realise in moving pictures, whose great strength is specificness and *vraisemblance*. This may explain why what we get on film or television screen is not Dickens. It may sound (at times) like Dickens. It may even look like Dickens. But Dickens it isn't. The overwhelmingly important thing is not the stories Dickens tells, but the way Dickens tells stories. It is a matter of verbal texture and point of view which cannot be realized on screen.

When Bitzer arrests young Tom Gradgrind, the boy's broken father asks: "Bitzer, have you a heart?" And his former star pupil "smiles at the oddity of the question." Acting cannot wholly convey the poignant irony of this moment. Or there is Pip's stolen piece of bread-and-butter: "Conscience is a dreadful thing when it accuses man or boy; but when, in the case of a boy, that secret burden co-operates with another secret burden down the leg of his trousers, it is... a great punishment." How could that be captured properly on film?

Another serious casualty is the comedy. From films and television it would be hard to realise that Dickens is one of the world's great masters of the comic. We have the impression that the Victorians were a miserable bunch. This may in large part be the result of those unsmiling contemporary time-exposure photographs, but we do approach Dickens somewhat solemnly. *Pickwick Papers* is one of the nation's supreme comic masterpieces, but much of the comedy arises not from the action – mistaken identities, confusion over bedrooms, false accusations of breach of promise and the like – but from the way things are narrated or described. Benjamin Allen asks Pickwick: "I say, old boy, where do you hang out?" and "Mr Pickwick replied that he was at present suspended at the George and Vulture." Comedy of this kind is untranslatable. Again, could acting recreate the unctuousness of Pecksniff, given us in Dickens' prose?

> It would be no description of Mr Pecksniff's gentleness of manner to adopt the common parlance, and say, that he looked at this moment as if butter wouldn't melt in his mouth. He rather looked as if any quantity might have been made out of him, by churning the milk of human kindness, as it poured upwards from his heart.
> *Martin Chuzzlewit*, Chapter 3

Then there is Vholes, the sinister lawyer in *Bleak House*, who takes off his close black gloves "as if he were skinning himself." It is said that as his long thin shadow on the outside of the coach, passes over all the sunny landscape, it chills the seed in the ground as it glides along. (*Bleak House* Chapter 35). This verbal felicity enables Dickens to be melo-dramatic and comic at the same time. When Marley's portentous ghost appears before Scrooge, his body is transparent, so that Scrooge "could see the two buttons on his coat behind" and "Scrooge had often heard it said that Marley had no bowels, but he had never believed it until now."

Such is the essence of Dickens' work, and it does not easily lend itself to realisation on screen. These are not bits of nourishing meat in a rich sauce. The meat and the sauce comprise a masterpiece. It is not the case that there are bits of comic or melodramatic action preserved in the aspic of Dickens' prose. The action and the prose in which it is embedded are one and inseparable, and have a life of their own which is uniquely literary:

> It was a numerous company, eighteen or twenty perhaps. Of these some five or six were ladies, who sat wedged together in a little phalanx by themselves. All the knives and forks were working away at a rate that was quite alarming; very few words were spoken; and everybody seemed to eat his utmost in self-defence, as if a famine were expected to set in before breakfast time tomorrow morning, and it had become high time to assert the first law of nature. The poultry, which may perhaps be considered to have formed the staple of the entertainment – for there was a turkey at the top, a pair of ducks at the bottom, and two fowls in the middle – disappeared as rapidly as if every bird had had the use of its wings, and had flown in desperation down a human throat. The oysters, stewed and pickled, leaped from their capacious reservoirs, and slid by scores into the mouths of the assembly. The sharpest pickles vanished, whole cucumbers at once, like sugar plums, and no man winked an eye. Great heaps of indigestible matter melted away as ice before the sun. It was a solemn and awful thing to see. Dyspeptic individuals bolted their food in wedges; feeding, not themselves, but broods of nightmares, who were continually standing at livery within them...
>
> *Martin Chuzzlewit*, Chapter 16

This is a comic scene, whose comicality comes to life only as we read it. The scene is comic not only for what is depicted, but for being constructed in our imaginations through the extraordinary perspectives set up in the language, and the numerous ideas and associations conjured up. The idea of mortal conflict is suggested by the term *phalanx*, which is further developed in the idea of *self-defence* and human preservation in asserting *the first law of nature*. The conceit of the slaughtered and cooked birds having a life of their own, and *taking flight down human throats* is an enchanting touch, climaxing in the sublimely ridiculous suggestion that they flew in *desperation*. The humour becomes ghoulish with the idea of nightmares *standing in livery* in the guests' overloaded insides.

The scene could be recreated visually in action in film or television terms, but devoid of its authorial voice, its comedy would be wholly different in kind.

The claim for cinematic qualities simply lacks evidence. It is asserted that because Dickens' fiction was originally published in serial parts, then it is eminently suitable for media-serial-treatment. That this childish assertion needs correcting is a sign of the state of media aesthetics as much as Dickens' criticism. This would only make sense if media serial episodes contained the same amount of narrative as the original chapter-parts, and were transmitted monthly over eighteen months (or in the case of *Hard Times*, *Great Expectations* etc, in weekly parts). But even leaving that aside, the zest seems to evaporate in film makers' hands. Nice sets, period costumes, and character actors working very hard for their money (sometimes, indeed, too hard) but to what minimal effect? But making them, and indeed going to see them, and speaking highly of them, seems to be a British quasi-religious ritual. The media have succeeded in creating a literary equivalent for Easy-Listening. The catalogue is not impressive.

George Cukor's *David Copperfield* (1934), David Lean's *Great Expectations* (1946) and *Oliver Twist* (1948), Alberto Cavalcanti's *Pickwick Papers* (1952), Ralph Thomas's *A Tale of Two Cities* (1958) and Christine Edzard's *Little Dorrit* (1987). Only *Great Expectations* is top of the league, and even here the guts have gone. The claim that Lean (who always filmed life like a tourist) realised Dickens' intentions must be resisted. The comicality and grotesquery have largely disappeared, to be replaced by a stultifying, genteel, prissy 'Quality Street' sense of period. Snobbery successfully masks Dickens' message – the destruction of personality by the ruthless mechanism of the class system. Lean's Pip is no working-class lad with gnarled hands and an unwashed accent. He is a nice little grammar school lad right from the start. The loss of the narrative voice entirely undercuts the irony.

There seems to be a failure of nerve when the media undertake filming or televising Dickens. Instead of using their means of production to tell us what he wanted us to know, they settle for marketing something which is perceived as 'Dickensian'. There is no reason, no principle, why translating a novel into another medium should be seen as trivialising it. Television is a language, with its own way of telling things. It could be used to say what Dickens felt needed saying. That this seldom happens reveals a great deal about class, education and the consumption of culture. Capitalism and cultural imperialism cause a packaging of the classics which renders them lifeless. Apparently, they sell well abroad – especially in the USA and the old colonial countries. But if the world thinks that it is getting Dickens on its screens, then the world is deceiving itself. But that cllective self-deception is what the author of *Great Expectations* has been trying to tell us about for many years.

Topography of a reputation

From our viewpoint at the start of the 21st century Charles Dickens seems to be a quintessential literary fact of the Victorian period. His vision is part of the way we actually define Victorianism, its reputation and construction.

Yet Charles Dickens was already a quarter century old, his fame established with *Pickwick Papers* and *Oliver Twist* before Victoria came to the throne, and he died over thirty years before the end of her reign. Such characteristically Victorian books as *Through The Looking Glass, Middlemarch, Under the Greenwood Tree, The Egoist, The Mayor of Casterbridge* were published after Dickens' death in June 1870. As a "great Victorian novelist" he was *not always there*. It took some years, and much critical effort, to secure him this position. There was much in-fighting, and a wide range of critical positions were to be canvassed before anything like the agreed academic acceptance we might easily take for granted today.

In the 125 years since his death Dickens' reputation has gone up and down – or, rather, down and then up. He was at one time the undisputed master novelist of his day: "nothing like it since Shakespeare" the formidable Lord Jeffrey said of *The Old Curiosity Shop*. But the tide was gradually turning against him – as far as the literary establishment was concerned – a decade before his death. Two things emerge in reading Victorian critics' comments about Dickens – the feeling that there was something which was not entirely gentlemanly about him (especially when he was compared with Thackeray) and the sense that his art was forced. Writing in 1862 George Lilly Craik, Professor of English at The Queen's University in Belfast, admitted that Dickens' novels dominated English fiction (along with those of Thackeray) but qualified this praise with some cautious comments which highlighted the absence of "unity of plot, or settled theory of life" in his novels, while admitting that while reading them the mind is possessed with the "illusion of reality":

Dickens had a great creative imagination – of the robust and grotesque kind certainly; and he could make both places and people apparent with extraordinary power. His pathos is often unbearable; his humour is inexhaustible and irresistible; his comprehension of life in its ideal aspects hardly exists at all.
George Lilly Craik: *Manual of English Literature*, 1862

It is important to note that Craik measured Dickens against Thackeray, whom he obviously regarded as a vastly superior novelist, possessing that requisite "definite theory of life" and

an attitude distinctly ironical yet as distinctly tender, now cynical, now sentimental, in which much real pessimism was made light and valorous by a sense of humour. Thackeray's people are instinct with that humanity which he at once satirizes and pities; and the style in which he reveals the secrets of their personalities is as nimble and expressive, as varying and sympathetic as his own emotional temper.

The young Henry James, writing in *The Nation* in 1865, said that Dickens had been forcing himself for the past ten years – *Bleak House*, *Little Dorrit* showed the strain, and *Our Mutual Friend* was "dug out with a spade and pickaxe." Only two years after his death, in an article in the *Fortnightly Review*, George Henry Lewes was already discerning that interesting divide which has so often characterised reception of Dickens' work – "immense popularity" and "critical contempt." Anthony Trollope, writing in his *Autobiography* 1882, drew a clear distinction between Dickens' ever growing popularity with all classes of readers, and his estimation among readers of taste and discrimination, who would avowedly place him at a lower level than Thackeray and George Eliot. Trollope sneered at Dickens, calling him "Mr Popular Sentiment."

At the close of the century, William Samuel Lilly asserted that *Pickwick Papers* was his masterpiece and that Dickens' was at his best in his earlier works, "where he makes small pretence to art" (*Four English Humourists*, 1895). Later Victorians found Dickens, attempts at large scale social-problem novels – the very kind modern critics admire the most – 'unreal'. In this respect Lilly is a very interesting witness, as he had heard Dickens read his works, and he stressed the equal success with which Dickens conveyed burlesque, caricature and pathos. He wondered whether anything bearing less appreciable relation to life was ever written than parts of *Our*

Mutual Friend. This would seem an eccentric opinion to hold today, when the later novels are so vastly preferred to the earlier fictions. By the end of the nineteenth century the reaction against Dickens had firmly set in, and significantly enough, the attitude had hardened particularly against his later works. The age felt itself superior to Dickens' vulgarity, and to bourgeois appeal. And the genius? The genius, the animating spirit which had conceived a whole world? It was a genius of the common mould, "it might have proceeded from a very superior bagman – a bagman of genius" according to Lilly. Apart from a few mavericks, such as George Gissing, Bernard Shaw and G.K. Chesterton, Lilly's views were shared by most critics at the beginning of the twentieth century. Even though Middleton Murray was predicting a return of Dickens to favour as early as the 1920s, the novelist's reputation was to reach its all time low in the decade before the Second World War.

Marxists and Freudians
Serious modern critical evaluation of Dickens dates from the end of the 1930s and can be seen being established in the publication of two outstanding and very influential works. Whatever their merits may be considered today, they are landmarks in Dickens studies. The first was T. A. Jackson's *Charles Dickens: The Progress of a Radical,* 1937, and the second was Edmund Wilson's *Dickens: The Two Scrooges* 1939. Whatever their shortcomings both these works demonstrated that Dickens was an author to be taken seriously. It was no longer bizarre to mention him in the same breath as Tolstoy, Dostoyevsky, Conrad, Kafka, Thomas Mann. This needed saying. Whether they realized it or not, these two critics founded the two main schools of modern Dickens criticism, which can still clearly be identified. The works of Jackson and Wilson are also important evidence of the profound effects on Dickens studies of two major developments in modern scholarship – the effects on our investigation of Dickens' achievement of Marxism and Freudianism, of politico-sociological studies and psychology. On one hand we had Jack Lindsay and Edgar Johnson, and on the other Warrington Winters, J. Hillis Miller and Taylor Stoehr.

Jackson's case, stated with the extreme brevity was that in most important respects except for his hope for the dictatorship of the proletariat, Dickens was a Marxist manqué. Jackson's emphasis then, was to concentrate on Dickens as a social critic, and to evaluate the exactitude of the novelist's social analysis. Thus was brought into vigorous life British socio-historical criticism, the tendency – in J. Hillis Miller's terms – "to dissolve Dickens' novels into the context of the social and political history of his time." Miller was referring to the work of Humphrey House, John Butt, Kathleen Tillotson. The danger was of heaping praise on creative work (*Hard Times* is frequently a case in point) in direct proportion to some politically correct scale of social values to the neglect of aesthetic evaluation.

Edmund Wilson concentrated on the psychology of Dickens' imagination. Wilson attempted to demonstrate that there were two aspects of Dickens: the benevolent/reforming and the criminal/destructive. Its main danger was the emphasis Wilson placed on the neurotic side of Dickens' mind. But his essay, *The Two Scrooges*, is a landmark – the beginning of psychological criticism of Dickens' work. Although this approach has been classically rebuffed by John Killham, in his essay on *Pickwick Papers* in John Gross and Gabriel Pearson's *Dickens and the Twentieth Century* (1962) and by Graham Smith's *Dickens, Money and Society* (1969) it does begin that characteristically "American" approach to Dickens so castigated by – among others – the Leavises:

> ... we have thought it essential to register specific protest against the trend of American criticism of Dickens, from Edmund Wilson onwards, as being in general wrong-headed, ill-informed in ways we have demonstrated, and essentially ignorant and misdirecting. In this connection we should perhaps explain our preference for Forster's *Life of Dickens* as a source, over modern, more 'correct' biographies, whether British or, still less acceptable, American...
> Preface, F.R. Leavis and Q.D. Leavis:
> *Dickens the* Novelist, 1970

All things to all men

Dickens seems to be one of those writers whom critics remake in their own image. We all seem to have a Dickens of our own, or at least, he seems to an extraordinary extent to be all things to all men. It does not take a very wide reading through the Dickens' critics to discern a wide range of Dickens' models are to be had off the peg. As suggested above, Edmund Wilson found him a tortured, schizophrenic-manic depressive and would-be criminal. But to G.K. Chesterton he was a cross between Father Christmas and Francis of Assisi. George Orwell found him a congenial political soul-mate, a friend to all he held in that idiosyncratic multi-mix emulsion of idealistic socialism he made his own – always campaigning about something:

> ...a man who is always fighting against something, but who fights in the open and is not frightened, the face of a man who is generously angry...a nineteenth century liberal, a free intelligence...
>
> *Inside the Whale*, 1940

To A.O.J. Cockshut ("How did a man with such a coarse mind become a master of his art?" is the question he brutally posed in *The Imagination of Dickens*, 1961) he is a totally inexplicable phenomenon, an ignorant "maker" chanting his wood-notes wild. For Dorothy Van Ghent, in a frequently reprinted article published originally in the *Sewanee Review* in 1950, Dickens was a trailer for Proust .Viewing him as an opponent of prison reform, an overt friend of the poor with marked snobbish tendencies, and quoting with obvious relish George Augustus Sala's dictum that Dickens was more Conservative than Democratic, Professor Philip Collins saw the allegedly "radical" Dickens as an old fashioned one-nation Tory (*Dickens and Crime* 1965). Many critics writing after the publication of Edmund Wilson's influential essay have firmly replaced the jolly Chestertonian philanthropical and convivial Dickens of the steaming punchbowl, glowing fireside at the stagecoach inn, of Sam Weller and Mr Micawber, with the dark, tortured Dostoyevskyan symbolist of dust-heaps and prisons. And we find that over ten years after Wilson's original 'impeachment' Professor Robert Stange of Washington University, St Louis, passed on Dickens a further 'Act of Attainder':

> Profound and suggestive as is Dickens' treatment of guilt and expiation in *Great Expectations*, to trace its remoter implications is to find something excessive and idiosyncratic... Dickens remarked to a friend that he felt always as if he were wanted by the police – 'irretrievably tainted' ...the Dickens of the later novels seems to be obsessed with guilt...

We might even anticipate that the cadence of the argument would be clinched with the magic name of the gloomy Russian master. We are not to be disappointed:

...Great Expectations... finds its analogues... in the writings of that other irretrievably tainted artist, Fyodor Dostoyevsky... 'Expectations Well Lost: Dickens' Fable for his Time' in *College English*, October 1954

This rather gloomy author is the Dickens of Lionel Trilling, Morton Dauwen Zabel, Jack Lindsay, Donald Fanger, Mark Spilka – where, for the most part, it seems very much to be a case of "for Dickens read 'Kafka'..." (See Fred Boege: 'Recent Criticism of Dickens', in *Nineteenth Century Fiction*, Volume 8, 1953).

Dr Leavis' change of heart

In the meantime, heralded by a public change of heart, Dr F.R. Leavis published *Dickens the Novelist* in 1970. In *The Great Tradition* (1948) Dr Leavis had argued that all roads led to D.H. Lawrence, and implied that the work of Fielding, Jane Austen, George Eliot, Henry James and Joseph Conrad had been in the nature of the ancient prophets preparing the way for the master, who was finally to manifest himself with *Sons and Lovers*. Life was too short to spend any time reading Fielding and J.B. Priestley, and Dickens, whose *Hard Times* alone was spared the flames, (was shoved into the grudging obscurity of an Appendix). Dr Leavis found that apart from *Hard Times*, Dickens' novels lacked "total significance of a profoundly serious kind" and the distinctive creative genius which controlled that "unifying and organising significance" which the truly great novelists always manifested. He admitted, that which indeed could never be denied, that Dickens works continued to be read, but believed his genius "was that of a great entertainer" who lacked the profound responsibility he expected of a creative artist: "The adult mind doesn't as a rule find in Dickens a challenge to an unusual and sustained seriousness."

The power of such negative criticism should not be underestimated. Like some kind of nerve gas, it paralysed the academic study of Dickens in Britain for a long time, certainly at Cambridge and further, for the Cambridge English School was extremely influential in the British education system for generations. Professor Philip Collins, one of Britain's leading academic Dickensians and at one time Head of the English Department at the University of Leicester, admitted in an article in *The Dickensian* published in May 1970 that he read no Dickens as an undergraduate at Cambridge "though the literary period which... attracted me was the Victorian..." Professor Collins' experience was by no means unusual. When I was an undergraduate in a very traditional British university during the 1950s, enjoying an English Honours degree course which in most other respects was wholly admirable, I was not offered a single lecture, tutorial or seminar on Dickens. And I, too, specialised in 19th century literature. But at the same time, across the other side of the Atlantic, Lionel Trilling was optimistically asserting that no one was any longer under illusion about Dickens, he was one of the two greatest English novelists "the other is Jane Austen." (Lionel Trilling: *A Gathering of Fugitives*, 1953)

Dr F.R. Leavis continued to reserve the right to doubt, but during the following decade there were significant signs of Dickens' rehabilitation. In 1962 he published a favourable critical essay on *Dombey and Son* in *The Sewannee Review* (which was to be reprinted as a chapter in *Dickens the Novelist*, 1970). In a letter to *The Spectator* (4 January 1963) he admitted he would "without hesitation surrender the whole *oeuvre* of Flaubert for *Dombey and Son* or *Little Dorrit*." In 1967, writing in the introduction to Peter Coveney's book *The Image of Childhood*, Dr Leavis described *Little Dorrit* as Dickens' "greatest work" and dilated on the need to get "the greatness of Dickens recognised as it ought to be." Dickens, he claimed, was "among the very greatest writers." Two years later in an article in the *Times Literary Supplement* (29 May 1969) he circulated the idea that the Immortal's stock had so far increased that he might be bracketed with Blake "who points forward to the Dickens of *Hard Times* (and not merely of *Hard Times*)."

In *Dickens the Novelist*, the famous *Hard Times* Appendix so successfully transplanted as a chapter in this new book, whose purpose, we were told, was to:

> ... enforce as unanswerably as possible the conviction that Dickens was one of the greatest of creative writers; that with the intelligence inherent in creative genius, he developed a fully conscious devotion to his art, becoming as a popular and fecund but yet profound, serious and wonderfully resourceful practising novelist, a master of it; and that, as such, he demands a critical attention he has not had...

Thus, a century after he fell to the floor at Gad's Hill, Charles Dickens gained academic acceptance.

Current state of play

Most early British academic studies of Dickens tended to the socio-political or historical context. Humphrey House published *The Dickens World* in 1941 and after well over half a century it has not been replaced. This book is not really about Dickens' fiction. It is about the context of fiction – the socio-economic and political world of the novels. This book remains one of the most useful attempts to locate Dickens' creative life in its social context. House's conclusion is that for all the claims for his radicalism, Dickens really followed rather than led public opinion. John Butt and Kathleen Tillotson's *Dickens at Work* (1957) explores the relationship between Dickens' imagination and the means of literary production. They reveal what a great step there is between what the novelist conceives in his imagination, and what finally appears in book form. The detailed examination of the surviving evidence accompanying several major examples of Dickens' fiction from first imagining to publication in book form is extremely revealing. Exploration of the novelists' notes, his correspondence, through a work's being commissioned, with instructions to illustrators, the effect of monthly or weekly serialisation, reaction by reviewers and readers etc. bring a greater apprehension of the nature of Dickens' genius. In 1962 Philip Collins published *Dickens and Crime*, which, while methodically rehearsing a very wide range of evidence in the fiction, journalism and public statements, tended seriously to undermine Dickens' reputation as a radical liberal reformer. Professor Collins's subsequent volume, *Dickens and Education* (1965), demonstrates that in the matter of educating children Dickens was far more liberal.

During the 1950s some of the most influential American work on Dickens started to appear. This tended to place more emphasis on showing how the fiction works on the imagination. J. Hillis Miller's *Dickens: The World of his Novels* (1958) is a landmark in this respect. This was the first major attempt to show the effectiveness of Dickens' symbolism, psychological insights and imaginative power entirely through his command of language, image and mythology. Reading this book now it is frequently difficult to believe that it appeared half a century go as it is clear how much subsequent modern work on Dickens J. Hillis Miller extraordinarily anticipated. Miller opposed the then fashionable assumption that the spirit of the age is responsible for the works of literature, and that works of literature become a symptom of the age and are altogether conditioned by it. His book saw Dickens' creative vision as in part determining the 'Victorian spirit' itself. He clearly identified two leading tendencies in literary criticism, either seeing a work as rooted in its age, in the life of its author and his theories of art and morality, and at the other extreme, the tendency to see a novel as a self-contained entity. What Miller attempted was to see a work of literature not as:

> ...the mere symptom or product of a pre-existent psychological condition, but as the very means by which a writer apprehends and, in some measure, creates himself. The given conditions of a writer's life, including his psychological nature as well as the culture he lives in, are merely the obstacles or materials which he transforms and vanquishes by turning them into novels or poems, that is, by giving them a different meaning from the one they had in themselves...

Although each major work is given full and separate treatment, this book put into circulation a conception of Dickens' fictions as unique, whole, coherent and entire – as a world of its own which comes to life as we read it. Reading Dickens after studying Miller one has to admit astonishment at how much in Dickens we missed the first time. For me, that is the greatest praise a reader can bestow on a critic.

Several critical works then continued what might be called the "new tradition" of concentrating on how Dickens' imagination worked, and how it achieves its extraordinary effects on readers' imaginations – A.O.J. Cockshut: *The Imagination of Dickens*, 1961, J.C. Reid: *The Hidden World of Dickens*, 1962, Earle Davis: *The Flint and the Flame – The Artistry of Dickens*, 1963, Robert Garis: *The Dickens Theatre – A Reassessment of the Novels*, 1965, Taylor Stoehr: *Dickens the Dreamer's Stance*, 1965, and William Axton: *Circle of Fire – Dickens' Vision and Style and the Popular Victorian Theatre*, 1966, are notable contributions in this respect. Among the most effective and wide-ranging contributions to this critical discussion was Steven Marcus: *Dickens – from Pickwick to Dombey*, 1964, which demonstrated that, properly handled, an awareness of the collective unconscious, of post-*Golden Bough* anthropological mythology, psychology and sociology could assist in evaluating Dickens' genius.

Two outstanding books appeared in the next ten years which contributed immeasurably to Dickens' restoration among the undoubted giants of literature. The first volume was *Dickens the Novelist* by F.R. Leavis and Q.D. Leavis which has been discussed above.

The second epoch-making book, *The Violent Effigy – A Study of Dickens' Imagination* (1974) by Professor John Carey, was a modest sized but extremely important study with the aim of demonstrating that:

> Dickens is infinitely greater than his critics. The point needs stressing because critics can, with unusual ease, appear intelligent at his expense. Shortcomings, ultimately irrelevant, in his own intelligence account for this, plus the presence of worthless elements in even his best novels. What makes him unique is the power of his imagination and, in Kafka's phrase, its "great, careless prodigality"...

Carey put the case that Dickens is "essentially a comic writer" and that this has usually been concealed because of the widespread literary suspicion that comedy, compared to tragedy, is light:

> ...comedy is felt to be artificial and escapist; tragedy, toughly real. The opposite view seems more accurate. Tragedy is tender to man's dignity and self-importance, and preserves the illusion that he is a noble creature. Comedy uncovers the absurd truth, which is why people are so afraid of being laughed at in real life. As we shall see, once Dickens starts laughing nothing is safe...

Plus ça change, plus c'est la même chose. This is where we came in with all those Victorians who so admired *Pickwick* and the earlier novels where Dickens made so little claim to 'art'. This was another, more determined (and more successful) attempt to answer that question so brutally posed by A.O.J. Cockshut: "How did a man with such a coarse mind become a master of his art?" Obviously in a book of little over a hundred and eighty pages not all aspects of this fascinating and important subject could be dealt with, and Professor Carey's particular interests and strengths were clear enough. His focus was particularly on the comedy, on Dickens' strange and haunting ability to make inanimate objects live and to make living things seem inanimate and on Dickens' essentially dualistic view of life – order/violence, radicalism/reaction, comedy/melodrama.

The abiding effects of the Freudian and Marxist inputs have indeed tended to emphasize the rather gloomier aspects of Dickens' art, and it was therefore welcome that Professor Carey concentrated attention on Dickens as a writer who functioned particularly creatively in comic mode.

He shed new and valuable light on Dickens' penetrating awareness of the frequent daftness of life and the endless comic resources of the English language in his hands. The power of the language seems to burn under his fingers as he manipulates it, leaping from association, redolence, ambiguity, pun, metaphor, image, emblem, *double-entendre* and sheer verbal felicity. This feature of his authorship is noticeable from the first, and it was a valuable contribution that Carey's book gave such attention to so much of Dickens' early work.

There is some overstatement of the case, however, as Professor Carey argues that Dickens' great strength in comedy accounts for the weakness of his grasp of the dramatic, with what he claims is an accompanying tendency to easily deteriorate into shallow melodrama. When Dickens' humour fails, he believes, "his imagination seldom survives more than a few sentences." This is demonstrably untrue. One need only recall the effective horror generated by the passage descriptive of Mr Dombey's journey to Leamington, to page after page of *Great Expectations*. Here Dickens is immensely successful and convincing in 'serious' writing, which works in context (this is an important point). We might grant that these passages are 'grotesque', but it must be insisted they are not humorous writing, nor failed comic writing.

Professor Carey also argues very persuasively for the recognition of Dickens' exploitation of what he terms "the border country" in Dickens' art – that fascinating area in his imaginative perception of life where things seem to come alive, where "coffins, waxworks, portraits, clothes, wooden legs" take on animation of their own. Here his insights are indeed impressive, though from time to time reminiscent of other, predominantly American, critics: "The course of things demonically possessed is to imitate the human, while the course of human possession is to imitate the inhuman. This transposition of attributes, producing a world like that of ballet, is the principle of relationship between things and people in the novels of Dickens..." wrote Dorothy Van Ghent in 1950. "Each object, each creature, animal or human, must be given a personality and a unique vitality" noted Robert Morse (*The Maturity of Dickens*, 1949). J. Hillis Miller stated that a "leap from reality metaphorically described to a world altogether fictive often takes place by a transition from simile to metaphor. Thus the Veneerings's butler is initially "like a gloomy Analytical Chemist"... but thereafter is simply "the Analytical Chemist." The character comes to exist entirely in the figure of speech which at first merely seemed to be a witty way to describe him..." (*Charles Dickens – The World of his Novels*, 1958). Steven Marcus comments of Mrs Gamp that "the energy of her identity... is so impressive that the clothes she wears retain her shape even when she isn't in them." (*Dickens – from Pickwick to Dombey*, 1961). Taylor Stoehr defines his ability to make "the physical surface speak for the inner condition. Pushed to its extremes, this is the opposite of dehumanisation; it is animism, another basically metonymic device in its dependence on the contiguity of characters and the objects which surround them..." (*Dickens: The Dreamer's Stance*, 1965). Nevertheless, although Dickens' animism seemed a new discovery to English reviewers, Professor Carey's book has been (and continues to be) one of the best contributions to Dickens criticism, in considerable part restoring the novelist's reputation as a master in the British poetic and comic tradition of Fielding, Smollett and Goldsmith and precursor of modernism and surrealism.

2   Dickens and the dream world

There is something special about Dickens' surrealism. It is surrealism quite unlike the surrealism of any other writer. It is utterly convincing, but convincing in essentially the same way that dreams are convincing. At the time, while we are in the midst of our dreams, we know they are not real, they are not 'true': but nevertheless as we experience them, we believingly inhabit them and take part in them. His fiction has the same qualities, and the same power. There is considerable reliable evidence that he had some kind of second sight, some awareness of other realities, that must not be ignored, and it might help us understand some aspects of his genius. One day Bulwer Lytton gave him the idea for a ghost story for *All the Year Round*. Unknown to Dickens, it was a true story, and the person to whom the incident had happened had promised it to another journal. It appeared in the 125th edition of *All the Year Round*. When the originator saw his story published in Dickens' journal, he quite understandably concluded that there had been treachery at his printer's. He wrote to Dickens and complained: "In particular", he demanded, "how else was it possible that the date, the 13th of September, could have been got at? For I never told the date, until I wrote it..." Dickens had looked through his version of the story and thought it would seem more authentic if it had a date, so he had added "September 13th."

He was not a racing man. He was taken to Doncaster races in 1857, and he bought a race card. Claiming (quite rightly) that he knew nothing whatever about racing form, he facetiously wrote down three names for the winners of three chief races: "And if you can believe it," he said afterwards, "without your hair standing on end, those three races were won one after another, by those three horses." In May 1863 Dickens dreamed that he saw a lady in a red shawl with her back to him. She turned round, and he did not recognise her, but she said to him: "I am Miss Napier." The next day, after a public reading, a lady was introduced to him in his retiring room by a friend of his. He recognised her at once as the lady of his dream. "Not Miss Napier?" he asked. Her name was indeed Napier. In the same year he seemed to have had premonition of the death of his son Walter in Calcutta. The occurrence is well documented. On the last night of December the family were playing Charades with all the children. He described what happened in a letter to Angela Burdett-Coutts:

...I had made something to carry, as the Goddess of Discord; and it came into my head as it stood against the wall while I was dressing, that it was like the dismal things that are carried at Funerals. I took a pair of scissors and cut away a quantity of black calico that was upon it, to remove this likeness. But while I was using it, I noticed that its shadow on the wall still had that resemblance, though the thing itself had not. And when I went to bed, it was in my bedroom, and still looked so like, that I took it to pieces before I went to sleep. All this would have been exactly the same, if poor Walter had not died that night...
Letter dated 12 February 1864

Walter Dickens died on 31 December, in Calcutta that same day, at a quarter past five, from an aneurysm of the aorta, with a gush of blood from the mouth. Dickens did not learn of the death of his son until the beginning of February 1864. One evening early in June 1870, the month in which he died, Dickens was talking to George Dolby, the manager of his reading tours, in the offices of *All the Year Round*. It was at the end of a day's work and Dolby noticed there were tears in Dickens' eyes. Dickens shook his hand and instead of wishing him "Good day" as usual, or "Good night" the novelist said, with particular earnestness, "Goodbye, Dolby, old man..."

We need only to be slightly acquainted with Dickens' work to know he was deeply interested in the 'other' world, the world of the supernatural, dreams, the occult. It was fashionable at that time, to be sure, but his interest is particular. His view of the 'other' world was not a simple one. He seems to have believed in its existence, but not to have believed that we could make direct contact through mediums and clairvoyants.

He wrote "I do not in the least pretend that such things are not ... I have not yet with any Ghost Story that was proved to me... I have always had a strong interest in the subject, and never knowingly lose an opportunity of pursuing it... Don't suppose that I am so bold... as to settle what can, and cannot be, after death..." (Letter dated 6 September 1859, addressed to Mrs Trollope). A few weeks later he wrote to William Howitt that he would willingly visit any proposed 'haunted house' and see for himself. (Letter 31 October 1859). His opinion of the commercial practitioners of 'Spiritualism' is perfectly clear: "My opinion of the whole party, is, that it is a combination of addle-headed persons, Toadies and Humbugs." (Letter dated 19 August 1859). He had "not the least belief in the awful unseen world being available for evening parties at so much per night..." (Letter dated 19 June 1855, to Mrs Trollope). But the books in his library at Gad's Hill testify to his abiding interest in such matters – Augustine Calmut's *The Phantom World, or The Philosophy of Spirits, Apparitions* etc, Catherine Crowe's *The Night Side of Nature, or Ghosts and Ghost Seers*, Walter Cooper's *The Philosophy of Mystery*, Joseph Ennemosr's *The History of Magic*, Charles Mackey's *Memoirs of Extraordinary Popular Delusions and the Madness of Crowds*, Robert MacLeish's *The Philosophy of Sleep* and F. Somner-Merryweather's *Glimmerings in the Dark, or Lights and Shadows*. Was Dickens just following contemporary taste when he serialised various works which dealt with the darker side of human psychology or with the supernatural, such as Wilkie Collins' *The Moonstone* and *The Woman in White*, Bulwer Lytton's *A Strange Story* and Robert Lytton's 'The Strange Disappearance of John Ackland' in *All the Year Round*?

Another aspect of his 'unworldly' psychologically supercharged or "otherworldly" qualities, I believe, is to be located in the apparently hypnotic effects of his public readings. Two things in particular stand out in Dickens' performances – his strange, uncannily compulsive power over the audience. Wherever he read, they would laugh, cry, roll about in the aisles, hold their breath, scream with fright, literally at his bidding. ("If you had seen Macready last night, undisguisedly sobbing and crying... you would have felt... what a thing it is to have power," he told his wife): and then there is his strange ability to assume character, to become in public view, in the space of a split second, another person – he was Bill

Sikes, Justice Stareleigh, Paul Dombey, Scrooge, and the audience believed they saw the very character, not Dickens 'pretending' to be Scrooge, but that Scrooge stood before them. He was himself conscious of this power, commenting after a Christmas reading in 1853: "They lost nothing, misinterpreted nothing, followed everything closely, laughed and cried with the most delightful earnestness, and animated me to that extent that I felt as if we were all bodily going up into the clouds together."

Everybody who went to these public readings noticed the extraordinary fixating qualities of his eyes. Some comments of Americans who witnessed his performances are preserved. They say his eyes were "like exclamation points" which "mingled kindness and sharpness" with "a look of keen intelligence about the strong brow and eye – the look of a man who has seen much and is wide awake to see more"; eyes "unlike anything before in our experience; there are no living eyes like them." (Quoted in Philip Collins: *Dickens: Interviews and Recollections*, 1981, volume 2, p300 ff). A certain Miss Cockran, who was determined not to be moved or 'taken in' by Dickens' performances, found that in person he was absolutely irresistible: "He is a wonderful magician" she said.

The idea that genius is close to madness, that sleep and dreams are closely related with the act of imaginative creativity, is an ancient and respected one. Coleridge's account of his dream-inspiration for *Kubla Khan* and its almost total evaporation when he was aroused is invariably called in to aid when such matters are discussed. In the genius there is something so demonic, so fiercely and energetically creative and rich that it sometimes seems only to be explained by association with an unbalanced personality. Dickens seems aware of such powers himself. "There is a drowsy state between sleeping and waking", he wrote in *Oliver Twist*, "when you dream more in five minutes with your eyes half open, and yourself half-conscious of everything that is passing around you, than you would in five nights with your eyes fast closed, and your senses wrapped in perfect unconsciousness. At such times, a mortal knows just enough of what his mind is doing, to form some glimmering conception of its mighty powers, its bounding from earth and spurning time and space, when freed from the restraint of its corporeal associate..."

The man who signed the contract to write *Pickwick Papers* with nothing particularly in mind at the time must have believed in the power of direct inspiration, as indeed he seems to have done. "I feel my power now more than ever I did," he wrote to John Forster on 2 November 1843, "That I know, if I have health, I could sustain my place in the minds of thinking men, though fifty writers started up tomorrow." He wrote to George Henry Lewes of a scene in *Oliver Twist* which had been particularly admired: "I thought that passage a good one when I wrote it... It came to me like all my other ideas ... ready-made to the point of the pen... and down it went..." He told John Forster during the composition of *Dombey and Son*: "I sit down to my book, some beneficent power shows it all to me, and tempts me to be interested, and I don't invent it – really do not – but see it, and write it down..." Curiously anticipating the theories of Jung he seemed aware of the richness of the subconscious and even the collective unconscious as the source for "all fable and allegory" – his words in a letter to Dr Stone (letter dated 2 February 1851).

Dickens must have thought deeply about the similarities between the world of the insane and the world the sane enter when they sleep and dream. He developed somewhere along the way towards a theory of the apparently collective nature of such mental experiences, with the power of universal themes, configurations of experience and character-types, such as became the province of Jung in our century. Dickens discussed these Jung-like ideas at some length in an article he wrote ten years later:

> Are not the sane and the insane equal at night as the sane lie a-dreaming? Are not all of us outside this hospital (he is writing of Bethlehem Hospital) who dream, more or less of the condition of those inside it, every night of our lives? Are we not nightly persuaded, as they daily are, that we associate preposterously with kings and queens, emperors and empresses, and notabilities of all sorts? Do we not nightly jumble events and personages and times and places, as these do daily? Are we not sometimes troubled by our own sleeping inconsistencies, and do we not vexedly try to account for them or excuse them, just as these do sometimes in respect of their waking delusions? Said an afflicted man to me, when I was last in a hospital like this: 'Sir, I can frequently fly'. I was half ashamed to reflect that so could I – by night. Said a woman to me, in the same occasion: 'Queen Victoria frequently comes to dine with me, and Her Majesty and I dine of peaches and macaroni in our night gowns, and His Royal Highness the Prince Consort does us the honour to make a third on horseback in a Field Marshall's uniform'. Could I refrain from reddening with consciousness when I remembered the amazing royal parties I myself have given (at night), the unaccountable viands I had

put on the table, and my extraordinary manner of conducting
myself on those distinguished occasions?"
'Night Walks' in *All the Year Round*, 21 July 1860

George Henry Lewes, writing in the *Fortnightly Review* in February
1872, predated Edmund Wilson, Warrington Winters and the Freudians
by many years when he wrote:

> Of him it may be said with less exaggeration than of most poets,
> that he was of 'imagination all compact'; if the other higher
> faculties were singularly deficient in him, this faculty was
> imperial. He was a seer of visions; and his visions were of objects
> at once familiar and potent. Psychologists will understand both
> the extent and the limitation of the remark, when I say that in
> another perfectly sane mind (Blake, I believe, was not perfectly
> sane) have I observed vividness of imagination approaching so
> closely to hallucination...

The emphasis on socioeconomic literary exegesis and the dominance
of Marxian critical theory has tended to over-estimate materialistic
considerations in studying Dickens, to the neglect of the psychological.
Not only does he noticeably draw upon and echo traditional sources such
as the *Arabian Nights*, myths and British fairy stories (references to which
abound in his fiction) but this archetypal material must affect the impact
of his fiction on readers. In part it may be explained by fashion. The
Arabian Nights had been introduced to English readers in 1707 through
an anonymous translation of a selection from Galland's French translation
(12 volumes 1704-17). Various English revisions and adaptations appeared
between 1785 and 1811. E.W. Lane's translation 1839-41, with additional
information about Arabian life arrived at a time when there was a vogue
for the exotic and found an avid readership. Dickens loved Lane's version
and read it constantly. Another exploitation of archetypal literary source
material which we know fascinated Dickens was the pantomime, which
was a flourishing and standard Victorian theatrical entertainment. There
are numerous references to pantomime stories in his novels, noticeably
to Dick Whittington and Robin Hood. Whittington and Cinderella themes
(Walter and Florence) are very strong in *Dombey and Son*. When we hear
something described as 'Dickensian' we are usually expected to understand
by it something quaint, old-fashioned, innocent, early Victorian,
Christmassy, jovial or grotesque. I would like to point to the quite different

qualities which in part made Dickens what he was, and indeed, is. It is no good thinking of him as 'Victorian' – for his work is quite different from Disraeli's, Thackeray's, George Eliot's, Trollope's, Hardy's, Kingsley's, Mrs Gaskell's – or any other Victorian novelist. It is the dream-like, other-worldly, almost mythical quality which makes his work stand out, and which gives it that haunting impact uniquely his and his alone. This has always reminded me of Oscar Wilde's interesting remark in *The Picture of Dorian Gray* (1891): "It is only shallow people who do not judge by appearances. The true mystery of the world is the visible, not the invisible".

Thomas Mann, writing of Freud, said that when a writer has acquired:

> ...the habit of regarding life as mythical and typical there comes a curious heightening of his artistic temper, a new refreshment to his perceiving and shaping powers, which otherwise occurs much later in life; for while in the life of the human race the mythical is an early and primitive stage, in the life of the individual it is a late and mature one. What is gained is an insight into the higher truth depicted in the actual; a smiling knowledge of the eternal, the ever-being and authentic...
>
> Thomas Mann: *Essays of Three Decades*, translated by
> H.T. Lowe-Porter, not dated, p422

Was Dickens' awareness of the other world the vital key which gave him access so early in his creative career to his feeling for and understanding of archetype, the permanent, unwritten, inherited unconscious mythology, the common property of the human imagination, which enabled him to communicate so directly to his readership, and to continue to do so generation after generation?

He certainly seemed to fear that the increasingly uniform and mechanistic qualities of industrial life would impact upon the sanctity of the human imagination. This is one of the reasons his treatment of modern city life is so impressive.

3   Dickens as City correspondent

Dickens was the first major novelist to take modern city life as his basic material. His novels do not use the cityscape as a background for the narrative action. It is more to the point to say that his novels – in the main – are actually about the modern city. Dickens consistently portrayed modern city life from early in his career when he commented on the faceless, anonymous quality of life which resulted from the crowding together of masses of people together in cities more or less required by the industrialisation and commercialisation of the economy. In 'Thoughts About People' in *Sketches by Boz* the young Dickens wrote:

> 'Tis strange with how little notice, good, bad or indifferent, a man may live and die in London. He awakens no sympathy in the breast of any single person; his existence is a matter of interest to no one but himself, and he cannot be said to be forgotten when he dies, for no one remembered him when he was alive...

When Mr Pickwick gets up on the first morning of his travels, he looks out of his window:

> ...upon the world beneath. Goswell Street was at his feet, Goswell Street was on his right hand, as far as the eye could reach, Goswell Street extended on his left; and the opposite side of Goswell Street was over the way...

When *Oliver Twist* is taken through London by Sikes in the journey preliminary to the robbery, his impressions are infernal – vacuous bustle, murk, anonymity, noise, smoke, a tumult of discordant sounds:

> It was market-morning. The ground was covered, nearly ankle-deep, with filth and mire; and a thick steam, perpetually rising from the reeking bodies of the cattle, and mingling with the fog, which seemed to rest upon the chimney-tops, hung heavily above. ...Countrymen, butchers, drovers, hawkers, boys, thieves, idlers, and vagabonds of every low grade, were mingled together in a dense mass...

The scene confounds his senses because of the hellish mixture of:

> ...the whistling of drovers, the barking of dogs, the bellowing and plunging of oxen, the bleating of sheep, the grunting and squeaking of pigs; the cries of hawkers, the shouts, oaths, and quarrelling on all sides; the ringing of bells and roar of voices, that issued from every public house; the crowding, pushing, driving, beating, whooping and yelling; the hideous and discordant din that resounded from every corner of the market;

and the unwashed, unshaven, squalid, and dirty figures constantly running to and fro, and bursting in and out of the throng...

In *Nicholas Nickleby*, Ralph Nickleby on his way home to hang himself after his final exposure, passes a graveyard. Here Dickens draws a parallel between the flesh and bones of the departed throng, the depressed, down-trodden exploited masses who have given up the struggle to make a living, and the living-dead, the busy, striving crowds of industrial, commercial, mechanised England. The cemetery is:

> ...a rank, unwholesome, rotten spot, where the very grass and weeds seemed, in their frowsty growth, to tell that they had sprung from paupers' bodies, and stuck their roots in the graves of men, sodden in steaming courts and drunken hungry dens. And here in truth they lay, parted from the living by a little earth and board or two – lay thick and close – corrupting in the body as they had in mind; a dense and squalid crowd. Here they lay, cheek by jowl with life: no deeper down than the feet of the throng that passed there every day...

Little Nell and her grandfather watch the crowded streets in the Midlands:

> The throng of people hurried by, in two opposite streams, with no symptom of cessation or exhaustion; intent upon their own affairs; and undisturbed in their business speculations, by the roar of carts and wagons... the two poor strangers, stunned and bewildered by the hurry they beheld but had no part in, looked mournfully on; feeling amidst the crowd a solitude which has no parallel but in the thirst of the shipwrecked mariner, who, tossed to and fro upon the billows of a mighty ocean, his red eyes blinded by looking on the water which hems in on every side, has not one drop to cool his burning tongue.

Long before the major satires of *Bleak House* and *Little Dorrit*, the idea of loneliness in the midst of the crowded city, of human anonymity, had been a leading theme in Dickens work. There are the stories 'Nobody's Story', 'Somebody's Luggage' in *The Christmas Stories*, and the original title of *Little Dorrit* had been *Nobody's Fault*. 'Nobody's Story' concludes:

> If you were ever in the Belgian villages near the field of Waterloo, you will have seen in some quiet little church, a monument erected

by the faithful companions in arms to the memory of Colonel A, Major B, Captains C, D and E, Lieutenants F and G, Ensigns H, I and J, seven non-commissioned officers, and one hundred and thirty who fell in the discharge of their duty.... The story of Nobody is the story of the rank and file of the earth. They bear their share of the battle; they have their part in the victory; they fall; they leave no name but in the mass...

'Nobody's Story', Christmas number, *Household Words*, 1853

In discussing the effects of the Crimean War on the British people, Dickens referred to:

We, the million, who have no individuality as a million, or as a corporation, or as a regiment, though as Mr A, or my Lord B, or Alderman C, or Private D, we each may suffer, and have our private griefs; we the Nobody Everybody, to whom nothing is anything to speak of...

Household Words, Volume IX, 1854

In his *Life of Charles Dickens* (1872), John Forster refers to ideas the novelist recorded in his notebook which might make the basis for development. Among them he recorded "a fancy that savours of the same mood of discontent political and social" as John Forster commented. Charles Dickens wrote:

How do I know that I, a man, am to learn from insects – unless it is to learn how little my littlenesses are? All that botheration in the hive about the queen bee, may be, in little, me and the Court Circular.

And another idea:

English landscape. The beautiful prospect, trim fields, clipped hedges, everything so neat and orderly, gardens, houses, roads. Where are the people who do all this? There must be a great many of them, to do it. Where are they all? And are they, too, so well kept and fair to see?

Life of Charles Dickens, Book IX, Chapter VII

Dickens is recording the same symptoms noted by Friedrich Engels. Modern industrial, commercial, city life crowded the striving together into a battle of life and death in which their common humanity was sacrificed as the strife was not only:

> ...between the different classes of society, but also between the individual members of these classes. Each is in the way of the other, and each seeks to crowd out all who are in his way. The workers are in constant competition among themselves as the members of the bourgeois among themselves...
>
> Friedrich Engels: *The Condition of the Working Class in England*, 1844, edited E.J. Hobsbawm, 1969, p108

Figures to support the Dickensian image of the crowded city as the centre of action in the novels are impressive. Throughout the period of Dickens' life the population not only increased, but concentrated itself in towns. The marvel of the nation's economic greatness, Engels proposed in the 1840s was really human sacrifice:

> After roaming the streets of the capital for a day or two, making headway with difficulty through the human turmoil... After visiting the slums of the metropolis, one realises for the first time that these Londoners have been forced to sacrifice the best qualities of their human nature ... The very turmoil of the streets has something against which human nature rebels. The hundreds of thousands of all classes... crowding past one another, are they not all human beings... with the same interest in being happy? And still they crowd by one another as though they had nothing in common...
>
> Engels: op. cit. pp57-8

As Frederic Schwarzbach argues in *Dickens and the City* (1979) Dickens' fiction plays an important part in the way we perceive the cultural impact of the growth of urban living. As Walter Bagehot remarked, Dickens described the city like "a special correspondent for posterity." Dickens' views were in the main representative of the consensus of enlightened public opinion, but Dickens himself moved from the country to the town at a time when it was a typical experience of the British – by 1851 only 49 percent of the population lived in the country – and in the notorious blacking factory episode he personally had childhood experience of industry. Hence it follows that Dickens individually experienced the great change from life in a predominantly rural economy to industrial and commercial city squalor. Frederic Schwarzbach goes on to argue that he created a myth of city life, still impressive to modern readers, by means of which to explore and evaluate this new experience.

Even though we have to admit Dickens' obvious love of the convivial and companionable qualities of town life (he missed the streets of London, vital to the stimulation of his imagination, when he was abroad) we may perceive a mythic structure in the famous autobiographical fragment which he wrote for John Forster – childhood/country/paradise as against adult-life/city/hell. We are looking at the myth of the fall from a lost rural paradise into the urban hell of infernal city. The myth is fairly well entrenched in British ideology. Dickens then, is writing in a tradition which stretches back to *Hesiod* and forward to *Cider with Rosie*.

This is not a theme just developed in the later 'serious' novels. We find it everywhere. In the chapter on the Hampton Races in *Nicholas Nickleby* he describes the grubby but glowing and cheerful faces of the gypsy children at the races, and underlines the contrast between these children of nature, and the maimed children of modern industrialised society:

> It was one of those scenes of life and animation, caught in its very brightest and freshest moment, which scarcely fail to please; for if the eye be tired of show and glare, or the ear be weary with a ceaseless round of noise, the one may repose, turn almost where it will, on eager, happy, and expectant faces... Even the sunburnt faces of gypsy children... suggest a drop of comfort. It is a pleasing thing to see the sun has been there; to know that the air and light are on them every day; to feel that they are children and lead children's lives; that if their pillows be damp, it is with the dews of Heaven, and not with tears; that the limbs of their girls are free, and that they are not crippled by distortions, imposing an unnatural and horrible penance upon their sex; that their lives are spent from day to day at least among the waving trees, and not in the midst of dreadful engines which make young children old before they know what childhood is, and give them the exhaustion and infirmity of age, without, like age, the privilege to die...
>
> *Nicholas Nickleby*, Chapter 50

He wrote to John Forster from Broadstairs on 16 August 1841:

I sit down to write to you without an atom of news to
communicate. Yes, I have something that will surprise you, who
are pent up in dark and dismal Lincoln's-Inn-Fields. It is the
brightest day you ever saw. The sun is sparkling on the water so
that I can hardly bear to look at it. The tide is in, and the fishing
boats are dancing like mad. Upon the green-topped cliffs the corn
is cut and piled in shocks; and thousands of butterflies are
fluttering about...

Thus he communicates his lively pleasure in the natural landscape
and in the novels he set out to celebrate what was warm, human, natural,
and his fear of the encroaching materialism, mammonism and mechanism
of Victorian life. We are bound to note that many of his evil characters
are associated with mechanism and calculation – Florence associates her
father with the sound of his squeaking footwear and ticking watch, Uncle
Pumplechook sets Pip complicated mental arithmetic tests, Mr Murdstone
thrashes David for his weak grasp of sums, Tom Gradgrind sticks to hard
facts, Mrs Skewton dies in pieces like a horrid old mechanical doll. By
contrast Mr Dick, whose advice saves David from returning to the
Murdstones, has lost his reason, Joe Gargery is illiterate, Captain Cuttle's
watch doesn't even tell the correct time.

Dickens was deeply shocked and disturbed by what he saw in the
industrial parts of England. What he read in various reports and details of
factory work and female and child labour he learned from such friends
and associates as Lord Ashley, the reformer, and Dr Southwood Smith,
the physician and reformer who helped to found the *Westminster Review*.
Dickens wrote of his visit to the Midlands in October 1838 that "miles of
cinder paths and blazing furnaces and roaring steam engines" loomed
through the fog and smoke like some enormous Alberich's cave of
clamorous glares, and that revealed "such a mass of dirt and gloom and
misery as yet I never beheld." He was particularly moved by evidence he
had read at the time he was composing *The Chimes* as to the failure of the
reformers to get a useful Bill through the Commons which would limit
the hours of work expected from female and child factory hands.

For Dickens the evil of modern society was centred in the city, and in
its alternative metaphoric sense, standing for the collective identity of all
the commodity trading, insurance business, stock-broking, trading and
commercial interests, as the City, which he saw as the antithesis of the
Celestial City. It was here that all interests were located, where decisions

were taken, investments made and commodities priced and humans reduced to commodities. Dickens' fiction is either about money and what it does to society or what it does to human beings. For Mr Micawber a modest error in an equation means misery. Barkis drifts out to eternity clutching his money box. Scrooge looks out of his window to a vision of the tortured of the damned in Afterlife, one of them chained to a monstrous safe. This is the wickedness Dickens characterises in the capitalists and utilitarians in *The Chimes*, and personifies in Scrooge, whose name is good enough upon the Exchange "for anything he chose to put his hand to" and in the merchant and capitalist Mr Dombey, "a pecuniary Duke of York." Flight from the city is a recurring theme in Dickens' work.

Smike and Nicholas look back on the city:

> It was by this time within an hour of noon, and although a dense vapour, still enveloped the city they had left, as if the very breath of its busy people hung over their schemes of gain and profit and found greater attraction there than in the quiet region above, in the open country it was clear and fair... A broad, fine, honest sun lighted up the green pastures and dimpled water with the semblance of summer... The ground seemed elastic under their feet...

The Eden theme runs right throughout Dickens' imagination:

> Pleasant, pleasant country, says Mr Pickwick, "Who could live to gaze from day to day on bricks and slates, who had once felt the influence of a scene like this? Who could continue to exist, where there are no cows, but the cows on the chimney posts; nothing redolent of Pan but pan-tiles; no crop but stone crop?"

What is Dingley Dell but a version of Eden? Little Nell flees the horrors of London and she traverses a pastoral landscape with her Grandfather, the West Country in *Martin Chuzzlewit* is idealised rural peace, Barnaby and his mother seek and find the haven of tranquillity in *Barnaby Rudge*. The Eden theme is comically but explicitly treated in *Martin Chuzzlewit*. This is a saga of a family motivated by cupidity. The wrapper of the serial numbers shows a face literally blinded by money, with coins in his eyes. Martin and Mark fruitlessly seek Eden, and fail to find it in America. Pecksniff, discovered in his garden, explains that his Eve has died but that he continues the work of Adam, the first gardener. The family is called together, to the City, and as Pecksniff is exposed and beaten to the ground by Old Martin, a book falls beside him. It is clearly *Paradise Lost*. We find it again in the tranquillity of Canterbury in *David Copperfield*. David associates his mother's picture with:

> ...the sunny streets of Canterbury, dozing... in the hot light; and with the sight of its old houses and gateways, and the stately, grey cathedral, with the rooks sailing round the towers...

He returns to the Kent of his happy childhood, which in his fiction represents peace, security and pre-industrial innocence:

> Coming into Canterbury, I loitered through the old streets with a sober pleasure that calmed my spirits... The venerable Cathedral towers, and the old jackdaws and rooks whose airy voices made them more retired than perfect silence would have done; and battered gateways once stuck full with statues... the ancient houses, the pastoral landscape of field, orchard, and garden; everywhere... I felt the same serene air, the same calm, thoughtful, softening spirit.

The ancient city of Lancaster is described in much the same terms in *The Lazy Tour of the Two Idle Apprentices* (1857). Cathedral towns seemed to offer him a kind of memory-stimulant of a wholesome, venerable past. Towers, cawing rooks, are a recurring group of images which to recall to his mind the peace, gentleness and good order of better times now gone. It doesn't matter if this 'Cockney pastoralism' is stereotyped, obvious or repetitious. What is important is the case was stated while such huge changes were happening in Manchester, London, Birmingham as so many Coketowns grew and spread like plague. Among almost the last words he wrote that June afternoon in 1870 we find presented once more that haunting image of the old English cathedral town:

> A brilliant morning shines in the old city. Its antiquities and ruins are surpassingly beautiful, with a lusty ivy gleaming in the sun, and the rich trees waving in the balmy air. Changes of glorious light from moving boughs, songs of birds, scents from the gardens, woods and fields – or rather, from the one great garden of the whole cultivated island in its yielding time – penetrate into the Cathedral ...and preach the Resurrection and the Life. The cold

grey tombs of centuries ago grow warm; and flecks of brightness
dart into the sternest marble corners of the building...
Edwin Drood, Chapter 13

But these matters are not organised in Dickens' work in an either/or
principle. Country and city are not viewed as simple alternatives. The
flight of Nell is a flight from the city, the city of death, and yet she dies
when she has reached the country. But it is in the city that such good
people as Kit, Dick, the Marchioness and Mr Witherden live. Further, we
have to explain the fascination that the death of Nell had on readers. (That
Nell should die was, incidentally, John Forster's suggestion). Freud is no
help here, for not all these fascinated readers had recently had their young
sisters-in-law die in their arms after coming home from the theatre. The
answer must lie in the deep appeal of traditional myth and fairytale, in
which Dickens' genius found harmonious accommodation. Nell is the
divine child of ancient mythology, who journeys through life and dies in
order to find perfection elsewhere, the golden child so fully documented
by Jung. It is all there – she is associated with the sun, her soul is
symbolised by her little bird, who takes flight as she dies. When Nell dies
she is surrounded by greenery and emblems of everlasting life. It is to the
tremendous pull of traditional myth that readers responded. *The Old
Curiosity Shop* is much more than a tract in the town/country debate of
last century England.

As the 1840s progress Dickens seems to be developing ideas of the
city as a modern social community, beneath the teeming surface of which
he discerns an organised complexity, symbolised by Todgers, which is
ancient, monumental, labyrinthine, enduring and teeming with life, like a
vital organ in the body politic of London:

> Surely there never was, in any other borough, city, or hamlet in
> the world, such a singular sort of place... And surely London, to
> judge from that part of it which hemmed Todger's round, and
> hustled it, and crushed it, and stuck its brick-and-mortar elbows
> into it, and kept the air from it, and stood perpetually between it
> and the light, was worthy of Todger's...
> *Martin Chuzzlewit*, Chapter 9

However grimy, eccentric and chaotic life seems at Todger's, it is a
bustling and lively centre of human activity and companionship. Whatever
the delays in serving dinner to their assembled guests "there was no hitch

in the conversation..."

Dombey and Son is not only a novel about capitalism and the power of money, but a novel about society as a system and man's relationship with the world. The action of this great novel coincides with Britain's early imperialism in Africa and India:

> Though the offices of *Dombey and Son* were within the liberties of the City of London... the Royal Exchange was close at hand; the Bank of England ...was their magnificent neighbour. Just around the corner stood the rich East India House. Anywhere in the immediate vicinity there might be seen pictures of ships speeding away at full sail to all parts of the world...

In Victorian schoolbooks might be seen the Gillray cartoon of European statesmen carving up the world like a huge plum pudding and the *Boy's Own Paper* showed young sailors handling the globe of the world as if it were a football. The badge of the Royal Marines was a brass world. Regimental battle honours featured the names of exotic places with strange sounding names – Jalalabad, Sindh, Natal, Kabul, Sutlej, Aliwal, Chilianwalah – exploits of British troops, conquering and policing an expanding empire which would be in the headlines at the time Dickens' novels were serialised. Mr Dombey is a symbolic figure of *homo economicus* at his imperial phase, at the stage when Europeans regarded the world as an object to be possessed and consumed. This was a new way of looking at the world, and Dombey, in his greed, his materialism, and his ambition, stands as a representative figure of Victorian capitalism and bodies forth its relationship with the world. It is no accident that Chapter 51 is called 'Mr Dombey and the World'. At the moment of the collapse of his business empire, his servants enact the ritual of consumerism:

> Misfortune in the family without feasting... couldn't be. Therefore, Cook tosses up a hot dish or two... and Mr Towlinson compounds a lobster salad... Even Mrs Pipchin... rings her bell, and sends down word that she requests to have that little bit of sweet bread that was left...

While Mr Dombey, "for he was proud yet... let the world go from him freely." *Dombey and Son* is a complex modern treatment of the dictum from St Matthew's gospel: "What is a man profited, if he shall gain the whole world, and lose his own soul?" The themes of capitalism and imperialism are not there to add colour to the novel – they are an essential part of Dickens' total imagining of the novel. An important fact to be faced, in reading this novel as a narrative about the 'City', is that for all the urging of Dickens' claimed anti-city attitudes, in *Dombey*, as in the story of Scrooge, he ultimately accepts capitalism as a system – *Dombey and Son*, as a firm, is continued into the next generation by Walter Gay. Scrooge becomes: "as good a friend, as good a master, and as good a man, as the good old city knew, or any other good old city, town or borough, in the good old world..."

Bleak House reflects Dickens' growing hatred of London. The emphasis here is not on the need for a mere patching-up operation to keep the whole system ticking over. The implications are more fundamental. *Hard Times* is more problematic, as possibly more than any other Dickens novel, it has been recreated to suit the ideology of more critics than any other.

Dickens regarded matters as far more complicated than simply damning industrialism as "evil." He was deeply conscious, in his awareness of widespread poverty, that it was essential people had work and the opportunity to work. This was why, when the evidence is actually consulted, and theories not just made up in the comfort of the liberals' armchairs and attributed to him, we can understand Dickens' motives for not readily supporting the ten hour proposals advocated by Lord Shaftesbury and his colleagues. Dickens was deeply uncomfortable at such efforts for change, fearing they might result in limiting people's chances to work:

> This question involves the whole subject of the condition of the mass of people in this country... and I greatly fear that until governments are honest, and Parliaments pure, and great men less considered, and small men more so, it is almost a cruelty to limit even the dreadful hours and wages of labour which at this time prevail. Want is so general, distress so great, and poverty so rampant – it is, in a word, so hard for the million to live by any means – that I scarcely know how we can step between them and one weekly farthing. The necessity of a mighty change, I can clearly see; and yet I cannot reconcile it to myself to reduce the earnings of any family – their means of existence being so very scant and spare...
>
> Letter to Dr Southwood Smith, 1 February 1840

Dickens' case, which is not compatible with the Marxist sociology once so strongly dominant in academic Eng. Lit. – is that harmonious relations between employers and workers are both possible and desirable, and that society as a whole would benefit from the wealth created by industry. With the knowledge of the terrible Miners' Strike of 1844 in his mind, and the strike of the Preston cotton operatives which he went personally to observe immediately prior to the composition of *Hard Times*, the novelist would have every reason to dread conflict and to hope for harmony. He loved humanity too much for it to be otherwise. I think Humphrey House and George Orwell are much safer analysts of this curious novel. It was written at a time when organised labour was hardly beginning, or, at least could not offer much industrial muscle to aid the plight of the worker. To encourage innocent men and women into open defiance of their employers (as Slackbridge attempts) was cruel and misguided as employers had enormous powers under the law. Consider these words penned by a contemporary about the strike of mineworkers:

> The strike had continued well on towards four months, and the mine-owners still had no prospect of getting the upper hand. One way, was, however, open to them. They remembered the cottage system. In July, notice to quit was served on the workers, and in a week, the whole 40,000 were put out of doors... The sick, the feeble, old men and little children, even women in childbirth, were mercilessly turned from their beds and cast in the roadside ditches. Soldiers and police in crowds were present, ready to fire at the first symptom of resistance...
> Friedrich Engels (*The Condition of the Working Class in England*, 1844)

4   Shades of the prison

For Dickens, civilised living essentially depends on getting things in proportion and properly balanced. *Little Dorrit* is not just about the dissolute city, it explores the curious human tendency to work things out, maintain an acceptable socio-equilibrium within the context of existence. The Marshalsea prison becomes a small world which generates its own system of governance. William Dorrit is the Father-of-the-Marshalsea, who survives upon a genial charity, is able to look down on his brother who plays a clarinet in the theatre. In *Great Expectations* Jagger's office, significantly, is situated in Little Britain. The parallels with Great Britain are obvious.

Wemmick remarks to Pip that hanging "is quite the natural end here, I assure you." It is Wemmick who manages a wholesome existence in London by balancing things out. The division of his personal-domestic life from the life of crime and lawlessness epitomises the way in which penal institutions and the power to punish become a permanent but hidden element in the fabric, structure and continuity of modern society. In early middle age Dickens gradually changed from an advocate for the complete abolition of hanging to opposition to public hanging. A Quaker abolitionist wished to enlist his name in aid of his campaign. Dickens answered:

> Distinguish if you please in quoting me between Public Executions and Capital Punishment. I would be glad to abolish both, if I knew what to do with the Savages of civilisation. As I do not, I would rid Society of them, when they shed blood, in a very solemn manner, but would bar the present audience.
>
> Letter dated 21 January 1864

Dickens gradually changed from his belief in the necessity of the total abolition of the death penalty to an acceptance of its social usefulness provided executions were not in public. This is paralleled in his view of developments in modern society where towns and cities work with much of their essential functions buried from awareness. Historically the change from feudalism, in which the physical body was owned by the governing class, to capitalism in which labour is by negotiation and contract, was paralleled by the development from the public exhibition of torture and execution as an essential part of the ritual of punishment as social control was gradually replaced by the secret processes of imprisonment and the spectatorless punishment of death. Modern torture is inflicted not on the body but upon the mind and the soul. The body as a target for vengeance disappears to be replaced by a widely reported public trial before a jury.

Prisons are hidden worlds in the midst of modern cities. The only way sanely to survive is to keep matters apart. Consider the compromise achieved by Wemmick, whose role in *Great Expectations* is symbolic, meant to represent the way we survive by compartmentalising our living. He lives a double life, part in the city, and part at home in his little fortified cottage. The two are kept as far apart as possible. As Wemmick tells Pip: "the office is one thing, and private life another." At his 'castle' in Walworth he can "brush the Newgate cobwebs away."

Dickens' message seems to be that although modern society makes torture, gibbets, gallows and pillories seem things from the past, we yet are far removed from the world imagined by the great reformers. The free world has perfected its own ways of conditioning our behaviour to the imperatives of commerce and industry. This may help us understand the disquieting similarities in our institutions. Prisons, schools, factories, barracks, hospitals – there is something disconcertingly alike in them all beneath superficial differences. Dickens gives us this uniformity in *Hard Times*:

> All the public inscriptions in the town were painted alike, in severe characters of black and white. The jail might have been the infirmary, the infirmary might have been the jail, the town hall might have been either, or both, or anything else, for anything that appeared to the contrary in the graces of their construction...

Dickens' fiction anticipated to a considerable extent the insights of Emile Durkheim, whose *The Division of Labour in Society*, 1893 detailed the socio-economic deep structures whose symptoms Dickens so convincingly portrays. Industrial capitalism brought a punitive system involving non-corporal punishment. This economic system demanded that the mind be disciplined and trained to accommodate human beings to the economic system's requirement for obedient, orderly, submissive routine behaviour. It has taken generations to produce conditions collectively referred to by teachers, politicians, employers and all the rest as "the real world." In a slave economy, there were punitive mechanisms to provide an additional labour force to supplement that provided by war and trading. In feudalism, at a time when money and production were at a primitive stage of development, there was a sudden increase in corporal punishments, the body being the only property accessible. With the development of the mercantile economy, forced labour and the prison factory appear, such as created the West Indian sugar industry. But the sophistication of the modern industrial system required a free market in labour. The century in which Charles Dickens was born witnessed the decline of forced labour exerted by punishment, replaced by corrective detention and highly disciplined attitude to work conditioned by the compulsory school system and youthful experience of the world of work. The new economic system brought an exchange of prisoners. Our bodies are freed but our souls are enslaved. This is why those scenes in *David*

Copperfield are so moving which detail young David's harsh treatment at the hands of Mr Murdstone as he tries to beat mathematics into him over a period of about six months. David's isolated, bullied state, his being shut out from his natural parent, would have rendered him stupefied:

> ...but for one circumstance. It was this. My father had left a small collection of books in a little room upstairs, to which I had access... From that blessed little room, Roderick Random, Peregrine Pickle, Humphrey Clinker, Tom Jones, the Vicar of Wakefield, Don Quixote, Gil Blas and Robinson Crusoe came out, a glorious host, to keep me company. They kept alive my fancy, and my hope of something beyond that time and place..."
>
> *David Copperfield*, Chapter 4

There are important details. We note that Murdstone takes him solemnly and ceremoniously upstairs for his thrashing, that he "had a delight in that formal parade of executing justice..." David is beaten "as if he would have beaten me to death." After his punishment, David sits in solitary confinement in his darkened room, wondering what further discipline might be in store for him: "Whether it was a criminal act that I had committed? Whether I was at all in danger of being hanged..." Like a convict, he is allowed "to walk in the garden for half-an-hour and no longer... I did so, and did so every morning of my imprisonment..." He is made to feel "a young outlaw" as he is allowed to stand near the drawing room door at evening prayers: "...to which I was escorted by Miss Murdstone after everyone was placed; where I was stationed, a young outlaw, all alone by myself near the door whence I was solemnly conducted by my jailer..."

His correction has hardly started. He is next sent to school, by way of preparation for the world of work at Murdstone and Grinby's. We cannot read these sections of the novel ("...no words can express the secret agony of my soul...") without being reminded of Dickens' humiliation at Warren's Blacking factory. This is bound to remind us of Wordsworth's lines in the *Immortality Ode* about "shades of the prison house."

David Copperfield impresses our imagination not because modern biography has revealed to us that such things actually happened to Dickens as a child, but because we respond to a work of literature which archetypically bodies forth universal experience of modern times. For all the period detail, Dickens addresses us as a contemporary.

Selected bibliography and recommended reading

A: Charles Dickens' works

Fiction
New Oxford Illustrated Dickens, twenty one volumes, (Oxford
University Press 1947-59)
Clarendon Dickens (Clarendon Press, from 1966)
World's Classics (Oxford University Press, from 1980)
Penguin Classics (Penguin Books, from 1980)
The Novels of Charles Dickens (J. M. Dent 1990)
Sikes and Nancy and Other Public Readings, edited by Philip Collins
  (Oxford University Press 1975)

Letters
Walter Dexter, editor, *The Letters of Charles Dickens* (Nonesuch 1938)
Walter Dexter, editor: *The Love Romance of Charles Dickens yold in
  his Letters to Maria Beadnell* (Argonaut Press 1936)
The Letters of Charles Dickens, edited by M. House and G. Storey
  (Pilgrim Edition, Clarendon Press, this edition is ongoing)
Edgar Johnson, editor: *The Letters of Charles Dickens to Angela
  Burdett-Coutts 1841-65* (Hamish Hamilton 1953)

Speeches
The Speeches of Charles Dickens, edited by K. J. Fielding (Clarendon
  Press, 1960)

Journalism
*The Uncollected Writings of Charles Dickens, from Household Words
  1850-1859*, edited by Harry Stone (Allen Lane, The Penguin Press
  1969)
Dickens' Journalism: *'Sketches by Boz' and Other Early Papers 1833-
  39*, edited by Michael Slater (J. M. Dent 1994)
Dicken' Journalism: *'The Amusements of the People' and Other
  Papers: Reports, Essays and Reviews 1834-51*, edited by Michael
  Slater (J. M. Dent 1996)
Dickens' Journalism: *'Gone Astray' and Other Papers from*

'*Household Words*' *1851-59*, edited by Michael Slater (J. M. Dent 1998)
Dickens' Journalism: 'Uncommercial Traveller' and Other Papers, edited by Michael Slater (Ohio State University Press 2000)
Charles Dickens: Selected Journalism 1850-70, edited by David Pascoe (Penguin 1997)

B: Biography

Peter Ackroyd: *Dickens* (Sinclair Stevenson 1990)
Arthur A. Adrian: *Georgina Hogarth and the Dickens Circle* (Oxford University Press 1957)
Philip Collins, editor: *Dickens Interviews and Recollections* (Macmillan 1981)
John Forster: *The Life of Charles Dickens 1872*, (edited by J. W. T. Ley 1927, revised by A. J. Hoppe, 2 volumes 1966, Dent Everyman 1966), (Penguin 1970)
Christopher Hibbert: *The Making of Charles Dickens* (Longman 1967)
Edgar Johnson: *Charles Dickens: His Tragedy and Triumph* (Hamish Hamilton, 2 volumes 1952: revised and abridged as one volume, Penguin 1977)
Fred Kaplan: *Dickens: A Biography* (New York, Murray 1988)
Norman and Jeanne MacKenzie: *Dickens: A Life* (Oxford University Press 1979)
Wolf Mankowitz: *Dickens of London* (Weidenfeld and Nicolson 1977)
Norman Page: *A Dickens Chronology* (Macmillan 1988)
Robert Patten: *Dickens and his Publishers* (Clarendon Press 1978)
Hesketh Pearson: *Charles Dickens: His Character, Comedy and Career* (Cassell 1992)
Una Pope-Hennessy: *Charles Dickens* (Chatto and Windus 1945)
Grahame Smith: *Charles Dickens; A Literary Life* (Macmillan 1996)
Michael Slater: *Dickens and Women* (Andre Deutsch 1983)
Claire Tomalin: *The Invisible Woman: The Story of Nelly Ternan and Charles Dickens* (Viking 1990)
Edward Wagenknecht: *The Man Charles Dickens: A Victorian Portrait* (University of Oklahoma Press1966)
Edward Wagenknecht: *Dickens and the Scandalmongers* (University of Oklahoma Press 1965)
Alexander Welsh: *From Copyright to Copperfield: The Identity of*

Dickens (Harvard University Press 1987)
Angus Wilson: *The World of Charles Dickens* (Penguin 1970)

C: Historical and social background

Charles Booth: *London Selections from Life and Labour of the People of London 1891-1903*, edited by Albert Fried and Richard Ellman, (Penguin 1969)
Asa Briggs: *Victorian People* (Odhams Press 1954; Penguin 1965)
Asa Briggs: *Victorian Cities* (Odhams Press 1963; Penguin 1968)
J.H. Buckley: *The Victorian Temper: A Study in Literary Culture* (Harvard University Press 1951)
Kellow Chesney: *The Victorian Underworld* (Temple Smith 1970)
G.D.H. Cole and Raymond Postgate: *The Common People* (Methuen 1956)
Philip Collins: *Dickens and Crime* (Macmillan 1962)
Peter Coveney: *The Image of Childhood* (Peregrine 1967)
Alan Delgado: *Victorian Entertainment* (David and Charles 1972)
H. Dyos and M. Wolff: *The Victorian City: Images and Reality* (Routledge and Kegan Paul 1973)
Royal Gettman: *A Victorian Publisher: A Study of the Bentley Papers* (Cambridge University Press 1960)
Robert Giddings: *The Author, the Book and the Reader* (Greenwich Exchange 1992)
Michael and Mollie Hardwick: *Dickens' England* (J.M. Dent 1970)
Fraser Harrison: *The Dark Angel: Aspects of Victorian Sexuality* (Fontana 1979)
W.E. Houghton: *The Victorian Frame of Mind 1830-1870* (Yale University Press 1957)
Humphrey House: *The Dickens World* (Oxford University Press 1942)
Louis James: *Fiction for the Working Man* (Penguin 1973)
Steven Marcus: *The Other Victorians* (New York , Basic Books 1966)
Henry Mayhew: *The Unknown Mayhew, Selections from the Morning Chronicle 1849-50*, edited by E. P. Thompson and Eileen Yeo, (Penguin 1971)
Henry Mayhew: *London's Underworld, Selections from London Labour and the London Poor*, Volume IV, edited by Peter Quennell, (Spring Books 1950)
Victor Neuburg: *Popular Literature: A History and a Guide* (Penguin

1977)

Robert Patten: *Charles Dickens and his Publishers* (Oxford University Press 1978)

Ronald Pearsall: *The Worm in the Bud: The World of Victorian Sexuality* (Weidenfeld and Nicolson 1969)

George Rowell: *The Victorian Theatre* (1956)

L.C.B. Seaman: *Victorian England: Aspects of English and Imperial History 1837-1901*, (1973)

Michael Slater, editor: *Dickens* (Chapman and Hall 1970)

Richard Southern: *The Victorian Theatre: A Pictorial Survey* (David and Charles 1970)

John Sutherland: *Victorian Novelists and Publishers* (Chicago University Press 1976)

John Sutherland: *Victorian Fiction: Writers, Publishers, Readers* (Macmillan 1995)

Kathleen Tillotson: *Novels of the Eighteen Forties* (Oxford University Press 1956)

David Trotter: *Circulation: Defoe, Dickens and the Economics of the Novel* (New York, St Martin's Press 1988)

Martha Vicunus: *Suffer and Be Still: Women in the Victorian Age* (1972)

Alexander Welsh: *The City of Dickens* (Clarendon Press 1971)

Raymond Williams: *Culture and Society 1780-1950* (Chatto and Windus 1958)

Raymond Williams: *The Long Revolution* (Chatto and Windus 1961)

Llewellyn Woodward: *The Age of Reform 1815-1870* (Clarendon Press 1987)

G.M. Young, editor: *Early Victorian England 1830-1865* (two volumes, 1934)

G.M. Young, editor: *Victorian England: Portrait of an Age* (1936)

D: Critical

William Axton: *Circle of Fire: Dickens' Vision and Style and the Popular Victorian Theatre* (University of Kentucky Press 1966)

John Butt and Kathleen Tillotson: *Dickens at Work* (Methuen 1968)

John Carey: *The Violent Effigy: The Imagination of a Novelist* (Blackwells 1974)

G.K. Chesterton: *Chesterton on Dickens: Criticisms and Appreciations of the Works of Charles Dickens* (J.M. Dent 1992)

Jane R. Cohen: *Charles Dickens and his Original Illustrators* (Ohio State University Press 1993)

Philip Collins (editor): *Dickens: The Critical Heritage* (Routledge and Kegan Paul 1971)

K. J. Fielding: *Charles Dickens: A Critical Introduction* (Longman 1958)

Raymond Fitzsimmons: *The Charles Dickens Show* (Geoffrey Bles, 1970)

George H. Ford and Lauriat Lane, editors: *The Dickens Critics* (Cornell University Press 1961)

Robert Giddings, editor: *The Changing World of Charles Dickens* (Vision Press 1983)

David Holbrook: *Charles Dickens and the Image of Women* (New York University Press 1990)

F.R. and Q. D. Leavis: *Dickens the Novelist* (Chatto and Windus 1970)

John Lucas: *The Melancholy Man: A Study of Dickens' Novels* (Methuen 1970)

John Lucas: *Charles Dickens: the Major Novels* (Penguin Critical Studies Series 1994)

Steven Marcus: *Dickens: From Pickwick to Dombey* (New York, Simon and Shuster 1965)

Jerome Meckier: *Hidden Rivalries in Victorian Fiction: Dickens, Realism and Re-evaluation* (University of Kentucky Press 1986)

Jerome Meckier: *Innocent Abroad: Charles Dickens' American Engagements* (University of Kentucky Press 1990)

J. Hillis Miller: *Charles Dickens: The World of his Novels* (Indiana University Press 1958)

Sylvere Monod: *Dickens the Novelist* (University of Oklahoma Press 1968)

Mildred Newcomb: *Imagined World of Charles Dickens* (Ohio State University Press 1993)

Anny Sadrin: *Parentage and Inheritance in the Novels of Charles Dickens* (Cambridge University Press 1995)

John Schad, editor: *Dickens Refigured: Bodies, Desires and Other Histories* (Manchester University Press 1996)

F. S. Schwarzbach: *Dickens and the City* (Athlone Press 1979)

Keith Selby: *How to Read a Charles Dickens Novel* (Macmillan 1989)

Grame Smith: *Dickens, Money and Society* (University of California
   Press 1970)
Taylor Stoehr: *Dickens: The Dreamer's Stance* (Cornell University
   Press 1965)
E. W. F. Tomlin, editor: *Charles Dickens 1812-1870: A Centenary
   Volume* (Weidenfeld and Nicolson 1970)

E: Reference

Arthur Hayward: *The Dickens Encyclopaedia* (Routledge and Kegan
   Paul 1969)
Michael and Mollie Hardwick: *The Charles Dickens Encyclopaedia*
   (Osprey 1973)
Paul Schlicke (editor): *Oxford Reader's Companion to Dickens*
   (Oxford University Press 1999)
John Sutherland: *Longman Companion to Victorian Fiction* (Longman
   1988)

OTHER BOOKS BY ROBERT GIDDINGS

The Tradition of Smollett
You Should See Me in Pyjamas (autobiography)
True Characters: Real People in Fiction (with Alan Bold)
Musical Quotations and Anecdotes
Who's Who in Fiction (with Alan Bold)
J.R.R. Tolkien: The Shores of Middle-earth (with Elizabeth Holland)
The Changing World of Charles Dickens
The Book of Rotters (with Alan Bold)
J.R.R. Tolkien: This Far Lane
Mark Twain: A Sumptuous Variety
The War Poets 1914-1918
Matthew Arnold: Between Two Worlds
Echoes of War
The Author, the Book and the Reader
Literature and Imperialism
Tobias Smollett
Screening the Novel (with Keith Selby and Chris Wensley)
Imperial Echoes
The Classic Novel: From Page to Screen (with Erica Sheen)
The Classic Serial on Television and Radio (with Keith Selby)

GREENWICH EXCHANGE BOOKS

STUDENT GUIDES

Greenwich Exchange Student Guides are critical studies of major or contemporary serious writers in English and selected European languages. The series is for the student, the teacher and 'common readers' and is an ideal resource for libraries. The *Times Educational Supplement (TES)* praised these books saying, "The style of these guides has a pressure of meaning behind it. Students should learn from that... If art is about selection, perception and taste, then this is it."

(ISBN prefix 1-871551- applies)
The series includes:
W. H. Auden by Stephen Wade (-36-6)
Balzac by Wendy Mercer (48-X)
William Blake by Peter Davies (-27-7)
The Brontës by Peter Davies (-24-2)
Joseph Conrad by Martin Seymour-Smith (-18-8)
William Cowper by Michael Thorn (-25-0)
Charles Dickens by Robert Giddings (-26-9)
John Donne by Sean Haldane (-23-4)
Thomas Hardy by Sean Haldane (-35-1)
Seamus Heaney by Warren Hope (-37-4)
Philip Larkin by Warren Hope (-35-8)
Laughter in the Dark - The Plays of Joe Orton by Arthur Burke (56-0)
Shakespeare's Non-Dramatic Poetry by Martin Seymour-Smith (22-6)
Shakespeare's Sonnets by Martin Seymour Smith (38-2)
Tobias Smollett by Robert Giddings (-21-8)
Alfred Lord Tennyson by Michael Thorn (-20-X)
Wordsworth by Andrew Keanie (57-9)

OTHER GREENWICH EXCHANGE BOOKS

Paperback unless otherwise stated.

English Language Skills *by Vera Hughes*
If you want to be sure, as a student, or in your business or personal life, that your written English is correct and up-to-date, this book is for you. Vera Hughes's aim is to help you remember the basic rules of spelling, grammar and punctuation. 'Noun', 'verb', 'subject', 'object' and 'adjective' are the only technical terms used. The book teaches the clear, accurate English required by the business and office world, coaching in acceptable current usage, and making the rules easier to remember.
With a degree in modern languages and trained as a legal secretary, Vera Hughes

went from the City into training with the retail industry before joining MSC as a Senior Training Advisor. As an experienced freelance trainer, she has worked at all levels throughout the UK and overseas, training business people in communication skills, but specialising in written business English. As former Regional Manager for RSA Examinations Board, she is also aware of the needs of students in schools and colleges. Her sound knowledge of English and her wide business experience are an ideal combination for a book about basic English language skills.
ISBN 1-871551-60-9; A5 size; 142pp

LITERATURE & BIOGRAPHY

The Author, the Book & the Reader by *Robert Giddings*
This collection of essays analyses the effects of changing technology and the attendant commercial pressures on literary styles and subject matter. Authors covered include Dickens, Smollett, Mark Twain, Dr Johnson, John Le Carré.
ISBN 1-871551-01-3; A5 size; 220pp; illus.

The Good That We Do by *John Lucas*
John Lucas's new book blends fiction, biography and social history in order to tell the story of the grandfather he never knew. Horace Kelly was born in Torquay in 1880 and died sixty years later, soon after the outbreak of the Second World War. Headteacher of a succession of elementary schools in impoverished areas of London during the first part of the 20th century, "Hod" Kelly was also a keen cricketer, a devotee of the music hall, and included among his friends the great Trade Union leader, Ernest Bevin. In telling the story of his life, Lucas has provided a fascinating range of insights into the lives of ordinary Londoners: their entertainments, domestic arrangements, experiences of the privations of war, including the aerial bombardments of 1917 and 1918, and their growing realisation during the 1920s and 1930s that they were doomed to suffer it all again. Threaded through is an account of such people's hunger for education, and of the different ways government, church and educational officialdom ministered to that hunger. *The Good That We Do* is both a study of one man and of a period when England changed, drastically and for ever.
ISBN 1-871551-54-4; A5 size, 213pp

In Pursuit of Lewis Carroll by *Raphael Shaberman*
Sherlock Holmes and the author uncover new evidence in their investigations into the mysterious life and writing of Lewis Carroll. They examine published works by Carroll that have been overlooked by previous commentators. A newly discovered poem, almost certainly by Carroll, is published here. Amongst many aspects of Carroll's highly complex personality, this book explores his relationship

with his parents, numerous child friends, and the formidable Mrs Liddell, mother of the immortal Alice.
ISBN 1-871551-13-7; 70% A4 size; 118pp; illus.

Laughter in the Dark – The Plays of Joe Orton *by Arthur Burke*

Arthur Burke examines the two facets of Joe Orton. Orton the playwright had a rare ability to delight and shock audiences with such outrageous farces as *Loot* and *What the Butler Saw*. Orton the man was a promiscuous homosexual caught up in a destructive relationship with a jealous and violent older man. In this study – often as irreverent as the plays themselves – Burke dissects Orton's comedy and traces the connection between the lifestyle and the work. Previously a television critic and comedian, Arthur Burke is a writer and journalist. He has published articles not only on Orton but also on Harold Pinter, John Osborne and many other leading modern dramatists.
ISBN 1-981551-56-0; A5 size 97pp

Liar! Liar!: Jack Kerouac – Novelist *by R. J. Ellis*

The fullest study of Jack Kerouac's fiction to date. It is the first book to devote an individual chapter to each and every one of his novels. *On the Road, Visions of Cody* and *The Subterraneans*, Kerouac's central masterpieces, are re-read indepth, in a new and exciting way. The books Kerouac himself saw as major elements of his spontaneous 'bop' odyssey, *Visions of Gerard* and *Doctor Sax*, are also strikingly reinterpreted, as are other, daringly innovative writings, like 'The Railroad Earth' and his 'try at a spontaneous *Finnegans Wake*'; *Old Angel Midnight*. Undeservedly neglected writings, such as *Tristessa* and *Big Sur*, are also analysed, alongside better known novels like *Dharma Bums* and *Desolation Angels*.

Liar! Liar! takes its title from the words of *Tristessa's* narrator, Jack, referring to himself. He also warns us 'I guess, I'm a liar, watch out!'. R. J. Ellis' study provocatively proposes that we need to take this warning seriously and, rather than reading Kerouac's novels simply as fictional versions of his life, focus just as much on the way the novels stand as variations on a series of ambiguously-represented themes: explorations of class, sexual identity, the French-Canadian Catholic confessional, and addiction in its hydra-headed modern forms. Ellis shows how Kerouac's deep anxieties in each of these arenas makes him an incisive commentator on his uncertain times and a bitingly honest self-critic, constantly attacking his narrators' 'vanities'.

R. J. Ellis is Professor of English and American Studies at the Nottingham Trent University. His commentaries on Beat writing have been frequently published, and his most recent book, a full modern edition of Harriet Wilson's *Our Nig*, the first ever novel by an African American woman, has been widely acclaimed.
ISBN 1-871551-53-6; A5 size; 295pp

Musical Offering *by Yolanthe Leigh*
In a series of vivid sketches, anecdotes and reflections, Yolanthe Leigh tells the story of her growing up in the Poland of the 1930s and the Second World War. These are poignant episodes of a child's first encounters with both the enchantments and the cruelties of the world; and from a later time, stark memories of the brutality of the Nazi invasion, and the hardships of student life in Warsaw under the Occupation. But most of all this is a record of inward development; passages of remarkable intensity and simplicity describe the girl's response to religion, to music, and to her discovery of philosophy.
The outcome is something unique, a book that eludes classification. In its own distinctive fashion, it creates a memorable picture of a highly perceptive and sensitive individual, set against a background of national tragedy.
ISBN 1-871551-46-3; A5 size 57pp

Norman Cameron *by Warren Hope*
Cameron's poetry was admired by Auden, celebrated by Dylan Thomas and valued by Robert Graves. He was described by Martin Seymour-Smith as: "one of... the most rewarding and pure poets of his generation..." and is at last given a full length biography. This eminently sociable man, who had periods of darkness and despair, wrote little poetry by comparison with others of his time, but always of a high and consistent quality – imaginative and profound.
ISBN 1-871551-05-6; A5 size; 221pp; illus.

Shakespeare's Non-Dramatic Poetry *by Martin Seymour-Smith*
In this study, completed shortly before his death in 1998, Martin Seymour-Smith sheds fresh light on two very different groups of Shakespeare's non-dramatic poems: the early and conventional *Venus and Adonis* and *The Rape of Lucrece*, and the highly personal *Sonnets*. He explains the genesis of the first two in the genre of Ovidian narrative poetry in which a young Elizabethan man of letters was expected to excel, and which was highly popular. In the *Sonnets* (his 1963 old-spelling edition of which is being reissued by Greenwich Exchange) he traces the mental journey of a man going through an acute psychological crisis as he faces up to the truth about his own unconventional sexuality.
It is a study which confronts those 'disagreeables' in the *Sonnets* which most critics have ignored.
ISBN 1-871551-22-6; A5 size; 84pp

Shakespeare's Sonnets *edited by Martin Seymour-Smith*
Martin Seymour-Smith's outstanding achievement lies in the field of literary biography and criticism. In 1963 he produced his comprehensive edition, in the old spelling, of *Shakespeare's Sonnets* (here revised and corrected by himself and Peter Davies in 1998). With its landmark introduction, it was praised by William Empson and John Dover Wilson. Stephen Spender said of him: "I greatly

admire Martin Seymour-Smith for the independence of his views and the great interest of his mind;" and both Robert Graves and Anthony Burgess described him as the leading critic of his time. His exegesis of the Sonnets remains unsurpassed.
ISBN 1-871551-38-2; A5 size; 200pp

POETRY

Adam's Thoughts in Winter by *Warren Hope*
Warren Hope's poems have appeared from time to time in a number of literary periodicals, pamphlets, and anthologies on both sides of the Atlantic. They appeal to lovers of poetry everywhere. His poems are brief, clear, frequently lyrical, characterised by wit, but often distinguished by tenderness. The poems gathered in this first book-length collection counter the brutalising ethos of contemporary life, speaking of and for the virtues of modesty, honesty, and gentleness in an individual, memorable way. Hope was born in Philadelphia where he raised his family and continues to live near there. He is the author of critical studies of Shakespeare and Larkin and is the biographer of Norman Cameron, the British poet and translator.
ISBN 1-871551-40-4; A5 size; 47pp

Baudelaire: Les Fleurs du Mal in English Verse
translated by F. W. Leakey
Selected poems from *Les Fleurs du Mal* are translated with parallel French texts, and designed to be read with pleasure by readers who have no French, as well as those practised in the French language.
F.W. Leakey is Emeritus Professor of French in the University of London. As a scholar, critic and teacher he has specialised in the work of Baudelaire for 50 years. He has published a number of books on Baudelaire.
ISBN 1-871551-10-2; A5 size; 153pp

Lines from the Stone Age by *Sean Haldane*
Reviewing Sean Haldane's 1992 volume *Desire in Belfast* Robert Nye wrote in *The Times* that "Haldane can be sure of his place among the English poets." The fact that his early volumes appeared in Canada and that he has earned his living by means other than literature have meant that this place is not yet a conspicuous one, although his poems have always had their circle of readers. The 60 previously unpublished poems of *Lines from the Stone Age* – 'lines of longing, terror, pride, lust and pain' – may widen this circle.
ISBN 1-871551-39-0; A5 size; 53pp

Wilderness by *Martin Seymour-Smith*
This is Seymour-Smith's first publication of his poetry for more than 20 years.

This collection of 36 poems is a fearless account of an inner life of love, frustration, guilt, laughter and the celebration of others. Best known to the general public as the author of the controversial and best selling *Hardy* (1994).
ISBN 1-871551-08-0; A5 size; 52pp

PHILOSOPHY

Deals and Ideals *by James Daly*
Alasdair MacIntyre writes of this book: "In his excellent earlier book *Marx: Justice and Dialectic* James Daly identified Marx's place in and extraordinary contribution to the moral debates of the modern era. Now he has put us even further in his debt not only by relating Marx to his Aristotelian predecessors and to the natural law tradition, but also by using this understanding of Marx to throw fresh light on the moral antagonism between Marx and individualist conceptions of human nature. This is a splendid sequel to his earlier work."
ISBN 1-87155-31-5; A5 size; 156pp

Marx: Justice and Dialectic *by James Daly*
Department of Scholastic Philosophy, Queen's University, Belfast.
James Daly shows the humane basis of Marx's thinking, rather than the imposed 'economic materialistic' views of many modern commentators. In particular he refutes the notion that for Marx, justice relates simply to the state of development of society at a particular time. Marx's views about justice and human relationships belong to the continuing traditions of moral thought in Europe.
ISBN 1-871551-28-5; A5 size; 144pp

The Philosophy of Whitehead *by T. E. Burke*
Department of Philosophy, University of Reading.
Dr Burke explores the main achievements of this philosopher, better known in the US than Britain. Whitehead, often remembered as Russell's tutor and collaborator on *Principia Mathematica*, was one of the few who had a grasp of relativity and its possible implications. His philosophical writings reflect his profound knowledge of mathematics and science. He was responsible for initiating process theology.
ISBN 1-871551-29-3; A5 size; 101pp

Questions of Platonism *by Ian Leask*
In a daring challenge to contemporary orthodoxy, Ian Leask subverts both Hegel and Heidegger by arguing for a radical re-evaluation of Platonism. Thus, while he traces a profoundly Platonic continuity between ancient Athens and 19th century Germany, the nature of this Platonism, he suggests, is neither 'totalizing' nor Hegelian but, instead, open-ended, 'incomplete' and oriented towards a divine goal beyond *logos* or any metaphysical structure. Such a re-evaluation exposes the deep anti-Platonism of Hegel's absolutizing of volitional subjectivity; it also

confirms Schelling as true modern heir to the 'constitutive incompletion' of Plato and Plotinus. By providing a more nuanced approach - refusing to accept either Hegel's self-serving account of 'Platonism' or the (equally totalizing) post-Heideggerian inversion of this narrative – Leask demonstrates the continued relevance of a genuine, 'finite' Platonic quest. Ian Leask teaches in the Department of Scholastic Philosophy at the Queen's University of Belfast.
ISBN 1-871551-32-3; A5 size; 154pp

FICTION
The Case of the Scarlet Woman – Sherlock Holmes and the Occult
by Watkin Jones
A haunted house, a mysterious kidnapping and a poet's demonic visions are just the beginnings of three connected cases that lead Sherlock Holmes into confrontation with the infamous black magician Aleister Crowley and, more sinisterly, his scorned Scarlet Woman.
The fact that Dr Watson did not publish details of these investigations is perhaps testament to the unspoken fear he and Holmes harboured for the supernatural. *The Case of the Scarlet Woman* convinced them both that some things cannot be explained by cold logic.
ISBN 1-871551-14-5; A5 size; 124pp

MISCELLANEOUS
Music Hall Warriors: A history of the Variety Artistes Federation
by Peter Honri
This is an unique and fascinating history of how vaudeville artistes formed the first effective actors' trade union in 1906 and then battled with the powerful owners of music halls to obtain fairer contracts. The story continues with the VAF dealing with performing rights, radio, and the advent of television. Peter Honri is the fourth generation of a vaudeville family. The book has a foreword by the Right Honourable John Major MP when he was Prime Minister – his father was a founder member of the VAF.
ISBN 1-871551-06-4; A4 size; 140pp; illus.